QUEERLY BELOVED

A LOVE STORY ACROSS GENDERS

Advance Praise for *Queerly Beloved*

"Can a relationship last when the person you thought you knew, is really someone different? Can it last when your partner transitions from one gender to the other? These are questions that are often asked, but sadly, very few narratives exist to reveal the answers, that is until *Queerly Beloved*. Diane and Jacob's love story and commitment to each other even in times of struggle and uncertainty will give readers hope when exploring their own relationships and the fear surrounding uncertain futures."—Ryan Sallans, Author of *Second Son: Transitioning Toward My Destiny, Love and Life*

"An important story to tell and book to read that highlights the many struggles the LGBT community faces and the complexities that comes with being queer. This is a wonderful patch in the broad and beautiful quilt that is the gay family!"—Perez Hilton

Visit us at www.boldstrokesbooks.com

By the Authors

Queerly Beloved: A Love Story Across Genders

The Blind Eye Detective Agency Series

Blind Curves

Blind Leap

Blind Faith

By Diane Anderson-Minshall

Punishment With Kisses

QUEERLY BELOVED

A LOVE STORY ACROSS GENDERS

by

Diane and Jacob Anderson-Minshall

2014

**QUEERLY BELOVED: A LOVE STORY
ACROSS GENDERS**

5573 6572 *off/14*

ISBN 13: 978-1-62639-062-1

This Trade Paperback Original Is Published By
Bold Strokes Books, Inc.
P.O. Box 249
Valley Falls, NY 12185

First Edition: May 2014

Credits
Editor: Shelley Thrasher
Production Design: Susan Ramundo
Cover Design By Sheri (graphicartist2020@hotmail.com)

Acknowledgments

Our relationship did not survive the events in this book in a vacuum. As a couple, we have benefited from the support of our family and friends including Athena and Jason Brewer, Erica Halberg, Dustina and Jennifer Haas-Lanier, Jeff Probart, all our parents (see the dedication), Wendy and Jose Cruz, Michelle and Rob Irwin, Keith and Tina Anderson, Tanya and Jaime Bolonos, Janet Engle, Tom and Ann Beyer, and the extended Anderson, Biggs, Norman, Minshall families.

Diane: I'd also like to thank Frances Stevens, my home girl and publisher at *Curve*, without whom my career would be in a different place today and without whose support Jacob and I might have gone into the closet about our relationship's biggest curveball. You standing by me during and after Jacob's transition made the world of difference to me. I also need to call out all the many brilliant women I've worked with over the years at *Curve, Alice,* and *Girlfriends*, the women who have sustained me creatively, supported me as a boss in a way I could never have dreamed possible, and who stood by me during and after the transition. To name just a few, among the dozens I could: Katie Peoples, Rachel Shatto, Kristin Smith, Stephanie Liang, Ondine Kilker, Flo Enriquez, Haley McMillan, Amy Silverman, Athena Brewer, Lori Selke, Kathleen Hildenband, and Bonnie Barrett. Lastly, a posthumous thanks to Helen Gurley Brown; though I never worked with her, she showed me an image of self-determined womanhood, and proof that a woman could be a career success, a sexual being, and a good wife without giving up her independence and self-determination. A note in which she congratulated me on launching my first magazine still hangs in my office. Today, I'd like to think she'd be proud of the queer woman I've become.

Jacob: The biggest callout for me should go to Max Wolf Valerio, Matt Kailey, Joshua Klip, Shawn Dorsey, Scott Turner Scofield, and all the other transgender men who helped me navigate through my transition. These guys, through their books, music, and other creative works, were instrumental in helping me figure out what manhood really meant to *me*. Thanks to all those who paved the way, the trans pioneers and people like Jamison Green, who kindly sat down with me years ago and showed me how much being a trans man was like anything else—simply what you decide to make of it. Helen Boyd Kramer deserves my thanks for not only giving voice to the partners of trans folk but for all the late night instant messaging, becoming my virtual friend and commiserating about non-feminists. We were experiencing the opposite sides of the same coin but continue to share many of the same feelings and experiences, and for that I am thankful. Thanks, too, to the brilliant trans women whose works (and personal words) have also added to my journey, including Jennifer Boylan, Julia Sereno, Ryka Aoki, Candis Cayne, Janet Mock, and Shawna Virago.

There are so many people we can't mention on this page, but really should. You probably know who you are and understand how brain dead and sleep deprived we are after finishing this book, and for that, we are most thankful. We couldn't have navigated this journey without all of your support, encouragement, and leadership. And lots and lots of coffee.

Dedication

To the village that raised us—Wayne and Judy Minshall,
Luanne Anderson, Keith and Marlene Foss Anderson,
Paula Hernandez and Bob Postel—for, in your own way,
helping us become the people we are. We've tried
to leave your stories out of this book as much as we could,
for your privacy and self-determination, though some day
we think they should be told, too.

INTRODUCTION

DIANE

Let me tell you about a woman I once loved. She was beautiful and unassuming, the kind of woman so used to thinking of herself as an ugly duckling that she doesn't even know how attractive she is. I saw a photo of her in high school once, about five years before I met her, and I couldn't believe she wasn't homecoming queen or most popular or something like that. She had dirty-blond hair in a rocker-girl shag and was wearing bell-bottom jeans (atop legs that seem to extend beyond what's reasonable) and a heavy-metal T-shirt. She was part Joan Jett and part Cherry Currie, but what popped out most (besides the killer legs, a fantastic body, and a smile that could melt icebergs) were her wolf-gray eyes. They were stunning in the photo and equally captivating the first time I could really gaze into them.

That first night it was just supposed to be about sex. It was a hookup. But she was funny and smart and eager to please, and one night (on her air mattress, in her graduate-student apartment) turned to two, then a weekend. I felt like I could stay in that bed forever (except it was an air mattress that kept deflating and had to be blown back up every four hours). Finally, the morning I was supposed to go home, go back to work, 240 miles away where I lived, I woke up to find her stroking my cheek, so softly, and gazing at me while I slept.

We moved in together almost immediately.

And she stayed smart and funny and gorgeous, and I watched her grow and change and develop as a person. From carny to press secretary, from construction worker to marketing guru, she kept changing, searching for herself.

Her look changed too. The hair got shorter, then shaggier, then buzzed, then shoulder length and pulled back into a constant ponytail. Her torn denim gave way to suits and then to the olive-green uniform and wide-brimmed hat that the park ranger on the Yogi Bear cartoons of our youth first made famous.

We'd stay up hours talking, debating really, politics and science, pop culture and low-brow art, the meaning of it all, what kind of people we wanted to be at twenty-five, thirty, forty, and if we lived long enough, even older. We couldn't fathom living that long. It just seemed so far off.

On the weekends we could make love all night, spoon half the day, and still find time to watch a movie and do some work. Even on the weekends we worked; we had to in order to get ahead.

She was always searching for something: the answer to meaning, her own meaning, a belief system that would explain who she was and how she felt. Sometimes I was all in—listening, learning—and other times I watched from a distance while she explored. Often she questioned and pondered and explored while I dove into work. Each of us had obsessions, and the meaning of it all felt like a luxury to me.

And she was sweet and caring and safe. She would check the locks on the doors ten times if I asked her, would charge after any loud bump in the night to make sure I felt safe. She was strong that way. And yet she was sensitive and vulnerable, always needing me—needing to be propped up, propelled, pushed forward into the brave new world.

Always she stayed model gorgeous. Kind of a butchy queer model, but tall and blond and beautiful. Or handsome. Both words would apply at different times.

Imagine this is the woman you love, loved for sixteen years. You were the perfect lesbian couple and nothing would ever shake your relationship.

Then she realized she was never that woman at all.

And you realized you were married to a dude.

That's my story. Here's how it all began.

JACOB (SUZY)

Diane and I are at QLiterati!, a monthly queer literary café we ran for a few years when we lived in Portland, Oregon. An older man is at the mic, reading a short story about a man on his way to have anonymous sex with a guy he knows only by the online handle bigdick25. This will be the protagonist's first time to have sex with another man. He's so excited he almost wrecks the car on his drive to their agreed-upon rendezvous destination, Portland's Forest Park.

But the man is also terrified. In fact, he's so scared that, in the end, he can't go through with it. He turns around and heads home. There his wife of thirty years, the mother of his adult children, is waiting for him. The man has never told his wife that he thinks he's actually gay, even though he's always sort of known. Now, decades into their marriage, he doesn't know how to broach the subject. After all this time, how does he start the conversation?

He's at a loss, but he feels like he can't keep living a lie. He doesn't realize it, but he's about to come out of the closet. By the time he gets home, his wife *knows*.

She's suspected for a long time that he's been keeping something from her. Afraid he's having an affair, she lets her curiosity finally overwhelm her respect for his privacy and reads his e-mail. She discovers his secret communications, the back-and-forth with bigdick25. The story seems like thinly veiled autobiography.

We're at the old Q Center on Water Avenue in Southeast Portland. Originally planned for retail, the building has ceiling-to-floor windows that originally struck me as an odd choice for an LGBTQ center. But it's 2008 and, fortunately, Portland's lesbian, gay, bisexual, trans, and queer folks aren't afraid of being seen.

The center's open-floor plan is now crowded with chairs—most of which are filled. The guests are all facing the back wall, where three chairs are set under a display of artwork. A microphone is set in front of bench, where the older man is perched, reading from typed pages.

QLiterati! (which can be pronounced as Q Literati, or—as I prefer, clit-er-ati) has quickly become a hit, and we regularly have sixty or seventy attendees. On this Wednesday night, one of our featured authors is Marc Acito, a funny, attractive guy who gained fame with his novel *How I Paid for College: A Novel of Sex, Theft, Friendship and Musical Theater*.

Before our guest authors read, emerging authors get a chance to share their work at an open mic. Most of the open-mic readers are repeat offenders, including our favorite gay pastry chef, Jason Zenobia, who always leaves the audience wiping away tears from laughing so hard.

But tonight is the first time the older man has signed up. When his turn comes, he walks to the microphone, sits on the stool, and begins to read from a paper in his hand. His story has the ring of authenticity. Every gay man can understand his urge to drive to that hookup that night.

During the Q&A period that followed the readings, the writer acknowledges that this was indeed a real experience. It happened to him a few years ago. But, he says, there's a happy ending: he has come out, gotten divorced, and now he's a proud gay man. The audience applauds. Marc Acitio jokes that *he* was bigdick25. They laugh.

I catch Diane's eye across the room. She's not laughing. She has a weak smile on her full red lips, but I can tell by the look in her greenish-brown eyes that rather than applauding his coming out, she's thinking about this man's wife, about how gut-wrenchingly painful it must have been for her. What it must have felt like to have the relationship she had invested *three decades* in crumble before her. How it felt to discover, after thirty years, that the man she loved wasn't the man she thought she'd married. That their relationship had been a lie. That he'd been keeping a secret from her all this time, that he'd been keeping perhaps the most important, essential part of himself hidden, that he'd never felt comfortable enough or loved enough to admit to her who he really was.

Diane isn't just imagining how it might have felt for that man's wife. Diane *knows* from firsthand experience. It was just three years earlier that she had gone through a similar experience, when, after fifteen years together, I finally admitted that I wasn't who I'd been pretending to be. Even though we'd only been together half the time the open-mic writer and his wife had, we would have thought we knew each other at least as well, if not better than they did.

In fact, we probably would have sworn we were way more honest and open with each other than most married couples. Yet my bombshell wasn't that different from his. The secret I had been carrying around was just as explosive and life-changing as the one he'd been hiding from *his* family.

DIANE

I saw it coming.

After fifteen years together I knew my life partner as well as I knew myself. I could predict what she was going to say before she said it. In fact, I'd been waiting for this day. I had been holding my breath for nearly six months, waiting for the other shoe to drop.

Suzy has always been a searcher, unlike me. I mean, I search for some things: a place to put down roots, the next big opportunity on my path to success, or a way to grow my family and bridge the gaps between lifestyle and geography.

But I've always known who I am.

Honestly, although I've grown and changed as much as anyone in twenty years, I imagine if you took me back in time and introduced the person I am now to the Payette High School class of 1986, they'd find I'm very much the person they knew then, albeit with some radical new political leanings (a far cry from my days as a young Republican).

But Suzy had always been trying to find herself, to understand herself, to know who she was. For her, that quest involved devouring endless books—self-help, spiritual, psychological, autobiographical, career, science—and talking to therapists, counselors, and advisors, or attending classes to learn whatever she thought might be her calling.

I remember for several months, a year or two after we launched *Girlfriends* magazine in the early 1990s, she went through shaman training in Half Moon Bay, California. Classes ran something like a hundred dollars a week, an ungodly amount at a time when we were living out of a tiny trailer on a San Gregorio horse farm, trying to make a living in the San Francisco Bay Area on something like twenty-four thousand a year.

Sure, she did some volunteer work with the teacher to reduce the costs, and she learned some things that she uses to this day (like meditation). And it was during a time in our lives when many of our friends were similarly engaged in slightly esoteric efforts to find themselves and decide what they wanted to be when they grew up. But it was her thing, not mine. I was never the kind of seeker she was.

A decade passed, and she was ten years older but still searching. But she was getting closer and closer to finding her truth. I could see the wheels turning in her mind. I could see that this time, it was more than just New Age musings, more than the other identities she'd tried on and quickly discarded. Something had clicked for her. And I knew we were living on borrowed time.

I feared that when she figured it out, it would mark the beginning of the end for our relationship. I didn't want to lose what we had. I didn't want to lose the person I'd loved for fifteen years.

Yet I realized I couldn't stop what was coming. And I wouldn't, even if I could.

I would wait for her to reach the point of clarity on her own, but once she had it, once she knew who she was, I could never have asked her to continue living what was, in essence, a lie. So I waited.

It took a long time. She approached it slowly, like navigating a labyrinth, spiraling closer and closer to the truth in the center.

It started with her saying, "Maybe, if I were younger, I would identify as..." She immersed herself in books with telltale titles like *The Riddle of Gender* and *From the Inside Out: Radical Gender Transformation, FTM and Beyond*. Finally she said the words: "I think I might be trans."

For fifteen years, the love of my life had been a girl named Suzy. Then she said the words I had been dreading, and—just like that—she was gone. She slipped away like a ghost fading into the night.

I still see her sometimes, brief glimpses of what once was. I used to occasionally tear up. The truth is, a small part of me misses her. A part of me always will.

But what I feared most didn't come to pass. We didn't break up. It hasn't always been easy, but we've made it through the transition as a couple. I lost a wife but I gained a husband.

JACOB

Back in the Q Center, Diane's eyes meet mine again. She gives me a wry smile. I nod and smile back.

So far—unlike the man and his wife—we're still together. It's 2008, three years since I came out as transgender. Maybe that's too soon to tell if we made it, if we survived the transition. But so far, at least, we're making it work.

So far, my beloved is still my beloved.

So far, so good.

❖

A 2011 report on a study by the National Center for Transgender Equality and the National Gay and Lesbian Task Force confirmed that those who transitioned from female to male (FTMs) were more likely to retain their relationships than those who transitioned from male to female (MTFs).

That could be because a strong percentage of FTMs were partnered with queer women, women who may find adjusting to a trans partner easier than a straight woman might. Straight women tend to have definite perspectives on masculinity, male-female dynamics, gender roles, and relationship etiquette that bisexual, lesbian, or sexually fluid women do not.

In other words, we couldn't have made it without Diane.

CHAPTER ONE

A DIFFERENT KIND OF WOMAN?

SUZY (JACOB)

Blame it on Arizona, or my cousins. Actually, it was my cousins in Arizona. I decided I *wasn't* a woman because my cousins *are*. Of course it wasn't as simple as that. These things never are. But what had been a tiny seed of doubt blossomed into a towering redwood after I spent time with them as adults. If they were women—and everything seemed to indicate they were—I didn't see how I could be. We were like two different species, the cousins and I.

It hadn't always been that way. The three Gilecki girls and we three Minshall girls met as kids at a family reunion. My older sister, Michele, hit it off with Belinda, the eldest. I hit it off with Terri, who, back then, seemed as much as a tomboy as I was. Bethany was the youngest. We kept in touch for a while, writing letters back and forth, but eventually we drifted apart, and twenty years came and went. Then, in February 2005, Diane was assigned a travel article that involved visiting a spa ranch resort in Arizona. My sister Michele, who'd been to see the cousins a few months earlier, convinced me to connect with the Gilecki girls and their mom, my Aunt Suzy, while I was in town.

Just before we left on the trip, a friend of ours found out she had to have a hysterectomy. She was younger than us, barely in her thirties, but she'd already been considering the operation for some time, as a preventative measure, because three of her aunts had died from uterine cancer.

Now doctors had found cancerous cells in her uterus and she was out of options. Afterward she'd have to start taking estrogen, but a lot of women had to do that once they hit menopause, so she felt it wasn't a big deal.

I thought about what I'd do in her position, or years later, when I started menopause. I'd be delighted to have my periods end, but I was far less certain I'd want doctors to put me on hormone-replacement therapy.

My mom had taken Premarin for many years and, ironically, had recently adopted a female draft horse previously owned by manufacturers of the drug. Along with thousands of other pregnant horses, this mare's urine was collected and turned into a hormone drug so human women wouldn't have hot flashes.

But a new, synthetic version of estrogen had begun outselling Premarin, after a large-scale clinical trial revealed long-term use of the latter increased the risk of strokes, heart attacks, and breast cancer. Drug companies no longer needed the mares they'd pressed into service. They started giving the horses away—no questions asked—to anyone willing to pay transportation costs from Canada.

When *my* body stopped making estrogen I didn't want to replace it. Not with mare urine, not with synthetic estrogen. I didn't want to intentionally feminize my body. I was having similar thoughts about breast cancer. My dad's mom had lost both breasts to cancer and wore a padded bra. Now most women were getting breast-reconstruction surgery after a mastectomy. But if I lost my breasts, I wouldn't go for that either. I'd just show off the scars like battle wounds.

That's what I was thinking in the spring of 2005 as Diane drove us through a desert landscape dotted with the distinctive silhouettes of many-armed Sargasso cacti. A storm hovered over our car, shrouding us in an eerie light.

Battered by wind and lit up by flashes of lightning, some of the passing Sargasso cacti were prickly torpedoes jutting into the sky sans branches, others stood with their arms outstretched like criminals being searched, others had many arms and seemed like strange, alien creatures. Despite their differences, though, all the cacti were clearly members of the same species.

I thought again about what makes us who we are. What makes us unique individuals?

We like to think we have free will and can become anything we'd like to. But in reality, we're restricted in what we can become. We have choices, sure, but our human possibility is limited by the potential of our genome and the environment—social, political and natural—in which we grow.

I was on my way to meet my Aunt Suzy, my namesake, and I wondered again what made me *me*. How much of who I was had already been predetermined, and how much could I control about who I was and would become?

❖

I met my Aunt Suzy and my cousins Belinda and Bethany at our hotel while Diane was off researching her article. They brought Buffalo chicken wings from Hooters. I couldn't believe they would eat at Hooters. (Although the wings *were* damn good, I've never eaten there since and never intend to. I still think they're a disgustingly sexist company.) But the cousins didn't seem to find anything wrong with it. They eat there all the time.

I was languishing in jeans and T-shirt, and although my clothes seemed perfect for eating Buffalo wings, I felt underdressed and out of place.

Belinda and Bethany were perfectly coiffed, darkly tanned, with the same big hair and serious makeup. A few days later, I met Terri, the cousin my age, the one who'd been a tomboy and seemed the most like me when we were young. Now she looked just like the other girls.

After my sister Michele had visited the Arizona cousins, she couldn't stop raving about how much they'd had in common, how much alike she and they were, even though they'd grown up in different states and taken different life paths. I could see it. The cousins reminded me of my sister. My aunt reminded me of my mother.

But none of them reminded me of me.

They talked about men and voting for Republicans and following major-league baseball and just who was taking over their neighborhoods, making them feel unsafe.

I nodded and smiled politely but felt like I'd been dropped on an alien planet. I couldn't understand what they were talking about. I couldn't fathom why they seemed to value the things they seemed to consider important.

I couldn't understand how Terri—a person I'd once identified with—had grown up to be so alien to me.

What had happened in the intervening decades to make us so different? Are our differences due more to the genes of their father or the fact that they grew up in Illinois and Arizona while I was in Idaho? Do they carry the scars of divorce? Does the particular religiosity of my parents make the critical difference between the Minshall girls and the Gilecki girls?

I'd always assumed I didn't fit with other women because I was a butch-identified dyke. But maybe it was more than that. I'd spent a decade arguing that I was just a different kind of woman. After my visit to Arizona, I started to really question whether I was a woman at all.

Maybe I wasn't a different kind of woman. Maybe I was a different kind of man.

❖

The rain stopped, and the air was fragrant with the post-rain scent and desert sands and flowers blooming. This area had experienced a drought for several years, and the rain was waking hibernating plants and flowers that sprang forth in a rush to life.

They would run through their entire lifecycles quickly during the brief respite from the arid heat of the desert landscape.

My Aunt Suzy said, "You have such a positive outlook on life."

I wanted to laugh. Instead, I muttered something like, "I've been kind of down the last few months." It was a gross under-exaggeration of the truth. I'd been in a deep, dark funk since April 2003, when an on-the-job accident cost me my park-ranger job and left me disabled and in agonizing pain.

It was devastating. I'd loved everything about being a ranger—the trucks and the uniform, hiking in the wilderness—and I missed it terribly, especially as I spent month after month lying on the floor staring at the ceiling.

Male coworkers expressed revulsion at my disability, confiding that their lives would be "over" if they were similarly injured. I seemed to make them uncomfortable. I had become the realization of their fears: injured, weakened, *feminized*.

When you stripped away my ranger uniform, I was no longer the person I imagined myself to be.

I had lost more than my job, more than the ranger residence we lived in, more than the former coworker friends who came by less and less often. I'd lost my independence, the ability to work outside of the house or do chores that required driving.

Eighteen months later when I could finally tolerate sitting, I was still limited to ten-minute segments and no more than three hours a day total. If Diane and I went to a movie, I'd leave her in the dark and pace theater halls. I'd drop back in, try standing for a few minutes, sit down again, get up ten minutes later and repeat the cycle. At restaurants I'd abandon Diane to walk or wait in the car.

I rarely left our tiny apartment except to walk our dogs. The only other people I interacted with were other dog parents, who often asked, "So, what do you do?" What did I do? I lay on the floor.

Work defines so much of our lives. For years I had identified first as a lesbian—everything else seemed subservient to that identity. But after I'd changed careers I'd started to identify *as* a ranger, and it had become my central identity. Now I'd lost it. I was no longer a ranger, and the lesbian identity no longer seemed like the home it once was.

Losing that masculine shell no doubt played a part in my recognition of my gender issues. I remember one of my aunts later warning me that it would be difficult to be a disabled man if I transitioned. But I found it more difficult to be a disabled woman. Something about having most of my masculine trappings stripped away made me even more uncomfortable with my femaleness.

In some ways it's not surprising that I recognized my trans gender identity after being injured. It's hard not to be present in your physicality when everything hurts. You do what you can to distract yourself. But ultimately the pain draws you back to your body. I could no longer escape my physical reality by throwing myself into work or engaging in masculine pastimes. Now I seemed defined by my body.

And the majority of my pain centered in my pelvic region. Sure I had sciatic pain down my left leg and arthritis in my neck, but the majority of the pain had its epicenter between my hips. Pain radiated out from that point like an earthquake, and it was the area of my body I was most psychologically uncomfortable with. Now it was also the most physically uncomfortable. With my days freed up from employment, all I had to focus on was that pain, that discomfort. Having lost my ranger identity, I was left searching for a new one.

CHAPTER TWO

DENIAL?

SUZY (JACOB)

For many trans people, the minute they discover that transitioning is possible they know it's right for them. That wasn't exactly how it was for me. I knew about the possibility of having what everyone used to call a sex change long before I self-identified as trans.

I was eighteen when I came out as a lesbian to my mom. It was 1985, and her first response was, "Are you sure you just don't want to become a man?" While that felt merely like a homophobic response, I admit it did acknowledge the existence of transgender men.

But I vehemently opposed the idea. It seemed ridiculous. In fact, the suggestion didn't seem authentic, rather more a gut reaction that demonstrated subconscious preference for my becoming a man and having a "normal" heterosexual relationship than staying female and having a relationship with another woman.

Following my denial, my mom wanted to know what had made me "that way." I wanted to know why being a lesbian couldn't be a choice. I mean, who wouldn't choose being with women over being with men? I loved everything about women. I couldn't imagine *choosing* to be with a man.

I also couldn't imagine choosing to *be* a man over being female. All my friends were women or gay men. I was a feminist. As a kid, I'd gone door-to-door with my mom, campaigning for the equal-rights amendment. I'd grown up during the women's movement. Men were the oppressors, the male chauvinist pigs, the people who had trapped women in marriages that made them little more than household servants.

Women seemed like the better sex. Women were the ones at the environmental protests and the equal-rights rallies. I really believed women were socialized to be better people. It was women who seemed to care most about social issues while men seemed to be the greedy people willing to oppress minorities and start wars and destroy the environment.

Later, during the 1990s, while I was still a lesbian, a mini explosion of trans awareness occurred, and for a while trans pioneers like Stafford traveled the talk-show circuit, gracing the stages of daytime talk shows and sparring with hosts like Maury Povich, Geraldo Rivera, and Jenny Jones.

But I remained oblivious. Even though we were in the trans hotspot of San Francisco—or, rather, living up to thirty miles outside of the city—I rarely watched TV, especially during the daytime. We had started *Girlfriends* magazine out of a tiny recreational trailer that had no TV, but even after we moved to an office in the city, we were so focused on promoting and growing the magazine we rarely paid attention to anything outside that work.

I don't actually recall what I thought of Stafford. I know I saw him during that period of time because I can recall his image: a tall, very Nordic blond man who looked a little like the Danish actress Brigitte Nielsen.

I do remember Loren Cameron and his self-portraits. A trans man, Cameron had completely transformed his body through testosterone shots and thousands of hours at the gym. He managed to sculpt a trim, muscular, body-builder physicality that rivaled wrestlers' physiques and proved that transgender men could—

with dedication and some good genes—achieve a scaled-down version of the Arnold Schwarzenegger or Sylvester Stallone brand of American masculinity.

Cameron produced a series of self-portraits in which he photographed himself in stereotypical masculine poses: smoking a cigar, wearing a hard hat, holding guns. While I respected his efforts to subvert and reclaim that kind of masculinity for transgender men, it was not the kind of masculinity I wanted for myself.

Cameron's self-focus reflected a similar introspective element in the 1990s FTM community, where creative portrayals of the FTM transformation seemed to verge on narcissistic. This may have been a natural, even useful stage in the development of a trans male culture and community, but it didn't capture my attention.

And even though I was becoming more aware of trans men in the 1990s, they didn't make me reconsider my gender. At that point, I didn't even consider the possibility of transitioning. During that time period Diane and I were busy starting and running *Girlfriends*, and I felt validated in my butch presentation. On my arm I had a sexy, totally stacked, long-haired, red-taloned femme that any straight guy would desire. I wore men's clothes and occasionally packed. I thought this is what it meant to be a butch, just as I thought Diane's tomboy childhood, assertiveness, and success-driven nature in the package of a classically feminine woman was what it meant to be femme.

Even when a friend announced that her partner, Sam, had decided to become a man, I didn't recognize myself within Sam's experience. Sam was older than I was and had always identified as a stone butch. She was an old-school butch, very much like the bar dykes I'd known in Boise, though Sam refused to be touched sexually. She wore a leather jacket, rode a motorcycle, and resonated with a level of masculinity I'd never managed to pull off myself.

Once I came out to myself, I wondered, "How could other FTMs transition right in front of my eyes and never once clue me in to the secret I was hiding from myself?"

I started to look back at my life through the lenses of gender-colored glasses, and suddenly I could read all the signposts and see all the clues and breadcrumbs I'd left for myself along the way. How could I not have seen them?

It's like in the *Matrix* when the endless, indecipherable strings of numbers and equations suddenly resolve into individual people and Neo can *see* the matrix. That's how my life looked to me, like it finally made sense—some of the choices I'd made, the places I'd felt uncomfortable, the times I'd sabotaged my own success and couldn't figure out why.

Suddenly I got it.

But, if it weren't for Diane, who knows if I'd ever have figured it out. Clearly, seeing counselors and shrinks hadn't led to the revelation, even if gender dysphoria *is* still considered a psychological problem in our society. As much as I wonder why *I* didn't see it, I also wonder why the mental-health professionals I visited over the years never noticed it either. (I'm not alone. My transition psychiatrist, Dr. Dea, admitted that she chided a shrink I'd seen before her for failing to see my gender dysphoria.)

Over the years, I've told therapists a variety of things that seem like they should have suggested I might be trans. I've said, "I always wanted to be a boy," "I wish I could be my father's son," "I wanted to prove I could take it like a man," "I never wanted breasts," and "Maybe my pelvic region hurts so much because that's the part of my body I hate the most."

But honestly I never said, "I think I'm really a man" or "I wish I had a penis."

Instead, even when I did finally talk about gender issues, I said, "I'd hate to be the woman who proves Freud right about penis envy."

I spent years in therapy trying to improve my feelings about my body. Usually therapists responded to my declarations of body dysmorphia by saying, "You know, it's not okay to hate parts of your body."

Unfortunately we live in a society where it isn't unusual for a woman to hate her body. Instead, for many women, hating their bodies is just a normal part of the experience of being female in America. No wonder it's difficult to diagnose such an aversion as a sign of transgenderism.

I didn't normally walk into a psychologist's office ready and willing to talk about my gender. Plus, since I was lesbian-identified, I still thought my gender was tied up with my sexuality. If the therapist or physician had tried to examine my gender identity, I'd probably have rejected their attempt as homophobic, as I did when my mother first questioned if I might want to be a man.

Unlike someone who has liver disease or gallstones, a person experiencing gender dysphoria (or what was called gender identity disorder until 2013) is probably the first person to realize it. Many mental-health providers aren't experienced with gender dysphoria, and it can take some transgender people years, or even decades, to come to the awareness ourselves.

In my case, being in the lesbian community and, in particular, being in a relationship with Diane helped postpone the gender issues that eventually bubbled to the surface. Diane was able to see me in a way that validated me, and because I found relative comfort within the role of a butch lesbian, I didn't feel pressured to transition.

Still, over the years, Diane and I had numerous discussions that began with her saying, "You know you're not a boy."

While this seemed like a clear factual statement, she repeated it regularly, as though I'd forgotten. Again.

I've always tended to shop for clothes in the boys' or men's section. I prefer their styles and want their clothes to work on me. But Diane recognized, many years before it finally dawned on me, that those clothes didn't fit the frame I'd been given. When I put on boys' clothes, they didn't make me look like a boy. If anything, they made me look more like a girl. I looked like I was wearing my father's clothes, like I was swimming in oversized shirts and suit coats.

So I stopped shopping in the men's section and agreed to wear clothes Diane chose for me that she believed would look the best draped on my form. Others were things she wanted to see me in, and still others were things she wished she could wear herself. Ironically, though I disliked my body, Diane always wished she'd had my long legs and thin thighs. (Over the years I've come to see that no matter how much you dislike what you have, someone else would give anything to have it.)

Because Diane wished she could wear clothes that looked good on my body type but not her own, at times I allowed myself to be her life-sized Barbie doll.

At least women's fashion trends created some pretty butch clothing, which made their way into my closet. Even if I still preferred my ranger uniform, Diane kept me stylish and fashionably butch, and I always loved that.

In addition to years in therapy trying to improve my feelings about my body, I tried other ways to embrace my femaleness.

I remember joining a women's circle but finding myself feeling out of place there too. I thought my alienation from these other women had to do with gender, but not the trans kind. I told myself we didn't see eye to eye because they were straight women and I was a butch-identified lesbian.

Here's another truism that took me a surprisingly long time to understand: while butch lesbians may be more masculine-identified than other women, they still tend to both accept and enjoy the fact that they *are* women.

And as great as I still think women are, I felt out of place in in a female body. I simply wasn't at home in my own skin, but I couldn't understand why or what that meant.

Was that denial?

DIANE

Like I said, I saw it coming. I could see the wheels turning for her. At this point Suzy was reading memoirs and short essays from other trans people. I realized this was more than just New Age musings, more than these other identities she'd tried on and quickly discarded. (And trust me, Suzy tried on many things in the search for identity, and as costly as it was or as tired of it as I got, I supported every damn one of them.)

But I knew something huge was coming. Something was clicking in her mind. I recognized it about six months before she did and was attuned to how much her attitude was shifting when it came to gender, toward transgender people and the trans experience. I kept wondering if I should bring it up or just wait, and in the end I decided to wait because this was going to be an experience I just couldn't control.

When we were very young, neither of us really understood what it meant to be trans. I know now that our ignorance led to a lot of ill-informed, perhaps even transphobic beliefs. For us, trans men seemed like they were rejecting feminism. We didn't know a lot of trans men, but those we did see on TV and around San Francisco seemed like misogynists who hated not just women, but any quality related to femaleness.

And something about lesbians becoming men and abandoning the queer community seemed like a betrayal; how could anyone relinquish their lesbian identity—something forged both in who and how we loved but also, for me, in the politics that surrounded us—in favor of being a man? I was a third-wave feminist who thought an awful like a lot of second-wave lesbian feminists: If you could choose to be with women, why wouldn't you?

I've heard others talk of this before—Olivia founder Judy Dlugacz and folksinger Holly Near—of the belief that there was something special about choosing to surround themselves with women. Judy even says she believed that once other women heard about this, they'd all choose lesbianism and the world would be a wonderful, peaceful one for us.

Alas, the hubris of youth might have been at play for all of us, but this was a time before the political and social conventions were, as they are now, firmly set in insistence that you have no choice in who and how you love, how you identify, who you are. I believed back then that you *could* choose and the smart choice was lesbianism, and those who I knew as lesbians who later came out as transgender men seemed to be rejecting all that we stood for. That was the betrayal I believed in then.

Although we didn't recognize it at the time, for Suzy part of that betrayal she felt was that she was sticking it out in the lesbian community, despite her difficulties. Why couldn't they?

When our friend Sam transitioned, she'd been an old-school stone butch, so her decision made sense to us. This was back before there was awareness that some stone butches were in fact transgender men. In the lesbian world, stone-butch women are tops sexually and they do not allow their partners to have any contact with their genitalia. They derive their pleasure from pleasing their partners, although some don't enjoy sex at all because it's a reminder of the genitalia they find incongruent with their masculinity.

At the time, that just didn't describe Suzy. She wasn't a top, and she certainly enjoyed an orgasm as much as the next person. I think she spent several hours flat on her back beneath me our very first night together.

In addition, we couldn't understand why anyone would want to exchange the queer community for the straight world. What a horrible trade-off, I thought. The LGBT community in the large cities where we'd lived was so vibrant and quirky and fun and sex-positive. This was before parenting and marriage filled the headlines of gay publications, and back then I thought of our community as more interesting and chic, more nightlife and politics, fewer play dates and PTA meetings.

But let's face it; we were lesbian-centric and straight-phobic. At the time, I think the only straight friends I had were Erica, a friend retained from high school, and Katie, one of my junior editors whom I adored. Both women have gay brothers, so they have queer cred in my book.

We were very uneducated about gender dysphoria and all the attendant psychological underpinnings of living in one body and identifying with another. Although we'd publically support trans men, at home we'd muse about just how someone could get to the point that they'd "mutilate" their bodies.

"Not me," we'd say in unison. "I'd *never* do that to my body." I've learned since that any time I begin a statement with "I'd never," at some point one of us will do whatever follows, even if it's years later.

Suzy seemed even more adamant. I mean, she embraced tattoos and always supported the rights of other people to do what they wanted with their bodies, but she secretly disapproved of most forms of body modification. She opposed nose jobs and breast augmentation and plastic surgery in general.

Perhaps there was an element of "thou protesteth too much." But that's not how I saw it at the time.

Or maybe it was really about growth and change. After all, I certainly know that my own perspective on plastic surgery has changed over the years. At forty-five I now understand why someone would choose certain beauty enhancements. But back when I had the taut skin and perky breasts of a twenty-two-year-old, I was clueless.

Things started really changing for Suzy in 2004, while I was editing the anthology *Becoming: Young Ideas on Gender, Identity, and Sexuality* with Gina de Vries. Several of the young contributors wrote about their gender issues and how they came to embrace a trans or genderqueer identity. As we started to read these stories and watch documentaries about transgender lives, heartfelt stories about the gender awakening and transitions of both young men and women, I noticed how Suzy was starting to change. Her attitude was more receptive and understanding.

"If I were younger," she said one day, "maybe I'd identify as trans." I started to hear the phrase more often, and I knew then that things were changing, even if Suzy didn't.

In our mid-thirties by now, both entrenched in the lesbian world, we considered transition more than a betrayal. It meant rejecting a community we'd helped establish with our work in LGBT media and our activism with groups like ACT UP and Queer Nation. How could Suzy now turn her back on all of that and reject our legacy?

And I couldn't help but wonder how her changing identity would impact my career and me. I was still invested in lesbian publishing. I'd been promoted to editor in chief of *Curve* magazine and was the happiest I'd ever been in my career. I loved my publisher, I loved my team, I loved the work we did. I was proud. And I was becoming an expert on television shows like *Secret Lives of Women* and *Lesbian Sex and Sexuality,* giving advice on everything from entertainment and fashion to dating and sex, but always from a lesbian perspective. I couldn't bear to lose it all.

I was a lesbian editor. I was a lesbian. I edited a lesbian magazine. How my readers saw me was as integral to my career success as the sixty hours I devoted each week were.

But I could see the change coming.

Although I'll always identify as female, I haven't always been a typical woman. You know how some women just want to vent when they complain, but they don't want you to solve anything? How they just want to be listened to? Women's magazines like *Cosmo* and *Glamour* have been telling me this is who women are for decades.

But that has never described me. I'm a problem solver. Exploring an issue, finding its causes and effects, searching for a solution can really irritate other people, especially other women who are, apparently, better at being women then I am. But I do like to resolve problems. And if someone's bitching about something, I usually assume that someone has a problem waiting to be solved.

So, when I was certain what was coming, when I saw Suzy's mind at work, my mind went to work too. I started planning how to solve the problem. When things clicked for her, I wanted to be prepared, like any good Girl Scout.

I didn't want us to be in limbo. I was terrified of losing my wife. Even though she'd worked in rugged jobs, wearing cute uniforms and doing jobs that were as butch as you could get (save for logging or staffing an Alaskan fishing boat), she had an essential femaleness I feared losing.

Like many of my female lovers, and certainly my ex-wife, Suzy had always been my physical ideal. I certainly loved her masculinity, from the beginning, but I also admit I did try to live vicariously through Suzy—buying her clothes that weren't as feminine as I'd wear but were, nonetheless, things I wished I were thin enough, tall enough to wear, like wildly patterned skinny capris. She was aware of my subversive efforts and was a good sport about it, sometimes wearing the clothes, sometimes laughing and poking fun at my ridiculousness.

For one of our earlier wedding ceremonies (it's a long story—we've had five total), I'd even talked her into wearing a white wedding gown that matched my own. I think she even wore pearl earrings that matched mine, no small feat considering she'd long ago let her pierced ears seal up from lack of use.

And as you would suspect, she was the center of attention there; the tall blonde in the beautiful gown prepackaged for a liberal media who wanted a "we're just like you" image to promote. Every TV news reporter there talked to us, though I was noticeably absent from much of the footage that aired. I assumed they edited me out of scenes for being too fat to be shown on network TV, an idea that had to have been permanently imprinted into my psyche years earlier when my teen dreams of becoming a broadcast journalist were dashed because—at a hundred and forty pounds—I was told I was simply "too fat for TV."

Anyway, I still cherish our photos from that ceremony, even if Jacob finds them laughable and ridiculous. It was, I think, only the second or third time Suzy had worn a dress, which only underscores the fact that she'd always felt uncomfortable with her own femininity. (By the way, two of those photos are on this book cover, our "before" shots that we thought long and hard about whether we could share with the world or not.)

When Suzy was injured she lost the job she loved. She adored everything about that job: the clothes, the trucks, being in the woods, fighting fires, clearing trails. After a lot of searching and discontent, doing everything from construction to accounting, publishing, landscaping, retail, and working on a low-rent traveling carnival, she'd finally found a career that felt like home. She might have been disillusioned with the organization she worked for, but she would always love the occupation of being a ranger. I could always see how happy and proud it made her to be a park ranger. She was devastated when she lost it because of a back injury.

Back then, we still dreamt that she might recover, given time. Maybe not enough to be a ranger again, but at least enough so she could transfer her skills to a related field, like working as a naturalist as a park or a tour manager at a wildlife area.

But that was contingent on recovery, and recovery didn't seem to be on the horizon.

She had lost her pathway to masculinity through her profession. Instead, she had to think about what it meant to be disabled, to experience how her lack of her job and her loss of independence feminized her.

So she read and she started seeing her own life script mirrored back to her. Before, she'd always interpreted her childhood feelings and experiences to mean she was a lesbian or a butch. But now she started to wonder.

SUZY (JACOB)

We returned to the San Francisco Bay Area from Arizona and visiting the cousins. A lot of stuff was percolating in my head. What did it mean to be a woman? In what ways had I not fit in with other women? I was copyediting Diane's anthology *Becoming: Young Ideas on Gender, Identity, and Sexuality* when I really began to *identify with* trans or genderqueer folks. I started saying things like, "If I'd been born a generation later, I'd probably be one of those trans bois."

At first, I really truly felt like I'd lost an opportunity, an option only available for the younger generation. I'd already missed that train, and I'd just have to wait for another lifetime to be a man.

But that started to change a few months later when *Bitch* magazine asked me to review a number of new transgender books, including *The Riddle of Gender: Science, Activism, and Transgender Rights* by Deborah Rudacille; and the FTM anthology, *From the Inside Out*, edited by Morty Diamond.

Everything began crystallizing for me as I read those works. Finally, I was seeing my own history reflected, my personal stories retold.

One of the first things I noticed about *From the Inside Out* was the number of queer contributors. Many of the trans men had gone from lesbian to gay following their transition. While that wasn't exactly my experience, it was the first time I was hearing from FTM men who had stayed involved in the LGBT community, post transition. This was very important to me because I didn't want to lose my connection with the community.

Something that several contributors mentioned as an aside was like a great revelation that I had simply never considered: butch lesbians may be more masculine-identified than other women, but they still tend to both accept and enjoy the fact that they *are* women. I'm not sure why this had never dawned on me before, but the small comment led me to consider the fact that perhaps I was not, in fact, just like other butch lesbians.

I also began to notice that a number of *From the Inside Out* contributors repeated some of my own concerns about some of the trans men who had gone before us. Like Wyatt Swindler who wrote, "Many trans guys devote a good deal of time trying to be taken correctly. Some have bought into what it means to be a Man as much as those socialized that way."

Then I read Reid Vanderburgh's contribution. Like me, Vanderburgh transitioned late in life; he was thirty-nine years old and had been living as a lesbian when he first recognized he would be happier living as a guy. He writes, "I did not take kindly to this realization, for several reasons. First, I had quite a life built up in the Portland, Oregon lesbian community. I was a founding member of nine years standing of the Portland lesbian choir and leaving that group was not on my horizon. Second, I had a family of choice with whom my bonds were stronger than those of my biological family. All were lesbians."

He shared my fear of losing that community if he transitioned.

Vanderburgh also acknowledged that "I'd never had conscious fantasies about being male. I had just never completely felt at home in my skin as a female, which caused the low-grade anxiety and depression."

And he shared my feminist background, as did Tom Kennard. Interviewed by Deborah Rudacille in her great scientific investigation into the changing landscape of gender, *The Riddle of Gender: Science, Activism, and Transgender Rights*, Kennard admitted it had been really difficult to become a man after decades as a lesbian feminist. "I was a big feminist, a white lesbian feminist, and I was kind of a separatist. I didn't like men, I didn't like the patriarchy, and I never wanted to grow up to be a straight white guy. I fought it for a long time."

Finally, a trans man was describing my own life and socio/political values. Part of Kennard's recollection of his youth—"I knew I was kind of different. But I didn't really know how I knew that"—also reflected my own, and he shared my concerns about being in a relationship with a woman and being invisible as a queer, being viewed as a straight couple invading queer space.

The personal stories in these books led me to re-examine my own life, my own memories, and even to reread the journals I kept when I was younger. Instead of looking at those experiences from the perspective of someone lesbian-identified, I tried to do so from the viewpoint of being transgender. And everything seemed to come into focus. I could see the breadcrumbs. I could see the Matrix.

From this new perspective, my life seemed to make more sense. When I was a little kid I looked like a little boy. I might have been born a girl, but my parents had pretty much allowed me to be as much a boy as I wanted to. Sure, they wouldn't let me play with toy guns, but they did buy me Matchbox cars and a cowboy action figure in place of Barbie. They let me wear boy clothes and cut my hair short and play with other boys.

I recall several circumstances where I wanted to play with a group of boys and they wouldn't let me because I wasn't a boy. I insisted I was a boy and they asked me a number of questions, sort of like a schoolyard version of a Turing test. I remember once being asked what color my underwear was (white) and, another time, which bathroom I used (the boys', on the left).

After my family moved out to a farm in Idaho, I was even freer to be a boy at home: I learned to shoot both a .22 rifle and a bow and arrow. I helped my dad build our corral, I helped my mom with the garden, I did chores, joined 4-H and raised animals, got into leatherwork and carpentry, and showed animals at the local fairs. Later during summers I hauled hay, harvested firewood from forests, and moved irrigation pipe like the other area country boys did.

Still, I rarely felt at home in my body. I've rarely thought of my body as me. It always seemed like another entity altogether, one that was often at odds, or even at war, with me.

I remember being jealous of my older sister's knees. Mine were bony whereas hers were wide. My kneecaps jutted out, and her knees seemed sturdier by comparison. I called hers "boys' knees" and mine "girls' knees."

Normal developmental changes only increased my sense of alienation with my body. It started doing things on its own. It wasn't in my control. It betrayed me.

When my breasts first began to form I thought something was wrong with me. I was so worried about the swelling of my chest that I told my sister, who told my mom, who took me to our pediatrician, who said this was normal. I was becoming a young lady.

I didn't want to be a young lady. I wanted to be a tomboy. I *was* a tomboy. I *wasn't* a young lady.

I went through the initial stages of grief: denial, anger, bargaining. It all seemed like a bad joke—me becoming a woman. I'd been a good kid. I'd read the Bible and believed in God, but my prayers seemed to fall on deaf ears. How could He do this to me?

When my period started I was certain I was dying. I had seen blood in the toilet after my mom went to the bathroom, and she had explained menstruation to us. Michele was already using tampons. But somehow I didn't put all that together when I started to bleed. Still, I didn't want to go see my doctor—who I had always adored as a child but who now seemed like a stranger because he thought breasts were natural for *me*. I couldn't bear the thought of anyone examining my private parts. So I didn't mention it to anyone. I took one of Jennye's old cloth diapers, cut it down to size, and waited to see if I died. I didn't.

I thought about these early experiences and how I felt at odds with my body, then combined them with other insights, such as those I've already mentioned and things like the way I had always avoided watching the movie *Boys Don't Cry* because Brandon Teena's life and death had always felt too close for comfort. Long before I identified as trans, I had been deeply impacted by his murder and had felt a level of kinship with him I couldn't entirely explain.

For me, all of this added up to only one thing: my gender was not normative.

I had determined that my gender fell along the transgender spectrum. But just because I had decided I was trans-identified, I didn't immediately understand exactly where on that spectrum I naturally belonged: was I genderqueer? Would I be satisfied just changing my name, or would I need to undergo a medical transition? Would I just take testosterone or would I pursue surgery? Although I had made this great leap in self-discovery, I still wasn't sure exactly what it was all going to mean.

By the time my *Bitch* review went to print, I was no longer Suzy. It was my first byline under my new name.

Though we had chosen my name days before, after a long search, to the rest of the world it seemed like almost overnight I became Jacob.

How did I socially transition overnight? My disability helped. I was still housebound by my chronic pain. So instead of going to a classroom or an office, I stayed and communicated with my boss electronically.

When I finished writing the *Bitch* trans anthologies review I e-mailed it to my editor, along with a note about how reading these books had opened a personal Pandora's box and I'd come to believe that I was myself transgender. Voilà, I was out at work. I also said that I would understand if the feminist publication would no longer want me as contributor once I became a man.

My editor responded with a note of congratulations, said they would always love to print my work, and asked if I wanted my name changed in time to correspond with the publication of the review.

The day I sent the first e-mail I was still Suzy. The following day, when I shared my new name with my *Bitch* editor, I had officially become Jacob. Abracadabra: I present to you the one-day transition.

JACOB (SUZY)

Some trans men attack their transitions like science projects, focused on their masculine presentations, rebuilding their gender presentation from the ground up. They observe cisgender men for hours and practice mimicking cisgender men's behavior: the way they walk, the way they talk, the way they hold their bodies, the way they take up space.

I'd learned from my communication classes that we all interpret these nonverbal cues and make subconscious—often instantaneous—assessments about people based on them. Many nonverbal cues are also relatively gendered in American society. For example, taking up more space projects power and a higher level of self-confidence. In the U.S., men are more likely to take up space than women: men tend to sit with their legs spread while women sit with their knees together.

Some trans guys practice for hours to get their performance down pat.

While considering transitioning, I wasn't interested in how someone might transform themselves from female to male. I just wanted to be comfortable as who I was. I didn't want to perform masculinity. I wanted to make my inner sense of masculinity become visible. I didn't want to have to change to come out trans.

I hadn't wanted to change when I first came out as a lesbian, either. I felt like coming out was supposed to just be an acknowledgment of one's true self; but of course, in reality, I *did* change after coming out as lesbian. I cut my hair. I embraced enculturation into the lesbian community.

So, I knew I'd change. But I didn't want to practice being male. I just wanted to be me in a male body.

After coming out as a trans guy, I didn't spend a lot of time focusing on or trying to alter my nonverbal cues. Although I've been told I could learn to lower my voice—which would certainly would help me pass on the phone—I never bothered to do so.

The truth is that now other people (especially men) often *do* sense that there is a difference in my gender presentation. But they don't generally make the connection that I'm trans. Instead, they tend to assume that I'm gay. And that doesn't bother me. In fact, I take it as a compliment.

But passing as a regular guy is very important for many (straight and queer) trans men. Some adopt the behavior of men who had been socialized in their gender from birth. They want to blend in with other guys and be typical American men.

I didn't.

As a feminist, what I didn't want was to be like just another straight guy. I didn't want to tell sexist jokes or take credit for women's ideas or laugh at fart jokes. I didn't want to watch football or forget my way around a kitchen or spend hours at a gym. I wanted to be as geeky and metrosexual and feminist as a man as I'd been before transitioning.

DIANE

Jacob was rather talky during this time, eager to discuss the ideas coming out of each of the books he read (many of which I read as well, sometimes even before he did). They weren't just memoirs, really; they were manuals for better living for him. Each one offered up the author's own hardships and pitfalls, elements that were perhaps more resonant at the time than the triumphs. By this point, you could Google "transgender" and "FTM" and find a host of blogs, and this same year (2005), after YouTube was launched, several FTMs posted video blogs of their transition, their pre-surgery/post-hormone bodies, and sort of moment-by-moment video updates of the things that many trans guys are excited most about (like the first facial hair, the deepening voice, the bulking up of muscles).

Jacob was excited about those things too, and so was I. I was a panoply of emotions, but one of them was excitement (and anticipation). Watching someone go through puberty in a condensed few months, thanks to biweekly testosterone shots, which is really what hormonal transition is like, makes you feel like you're helping usher a new person into the world.

The arduous wait for facial hair turned into a full goatee in no time, though I had to help him learn to shape it properly. I bought him new clothes, took him to a barber, and, most importantly, tried to imbue some sense of what manners were expected of him. It's funny because I'm not a woman who needs a door opened for me, but I'm aware of the expectations that men open doors. I'm aware of social conventions. So early on I was constantly frustrated when Jacob didn't just know what all these male social expectations were, like opening doors, letting women exit the elevator first (and holding the door), standing when a woman enters a room, and so on. It might seem old fashioned, but social convention decrees that many of those things still happen, at least in some circumstances, and if a guy doesn't do them, he just seems like an asshole. I tried very hard to not let my new husband become an asshole. I said the phrase, "It makes you seem like a douche" more than once.

Since Jacob grew up on a farm, he just wasn't aware of a certain amount of social etiquette because it wasn't a part of his life. He could raise a prize pig, run six miles at a champion rate, and ace a science midterm, but he couldn't tell you why there were four forks on a place setting at dinnertime. That stuff just didn't matter at the farm, and because he wasn't enculturated as a male, he didn't learn the things men were supposed to just know, like holding a restaurant door open when women are standing there.

But he's always loved a research project, and so a lot of the knowledge he got about the many ways that trans men become men—and how they identify and live and act—was like one big research project. If there had been a test somewhere along the way, he would no doubt have aced it. Except for one thing: I could still never get him to watch *Boys Don't Cry*. It's a film that I think is one of the ten best LGBTQ films of all time, and its beauty in tragedy should serve as a reminder to someone like Jacob of the sheer privilege he's had in his transition. Brandon Teena, the real-life trans man who is killed in the film, didn't have a supportive family, health coverage, or access to therapy or trans resources. He was both stuck in his circumstances, barely knowing how to define himself, much less being able to really share that confusion with the world. And his quest for belonging, for friends and family, turned into the kind of violence that no one should ever have to suffer.

During Jacob's first few visits to public men's rooms, I thought about that movie every single time as I waited for him to come out. Once, after frothing myself into a panic because it had been so long, I walked into a public restroom at a highway rest stop and yelled his name. He was fine, and eventually I would be too.

CHAPTER THREE

THE ROAD TO MANHOOD

DIANE

By the time Jacob told me he felt like a man, I was ready. Of course I was also terrified and sad for me, but I had a plan in place. I pushed Jacob to get into therapy immediately, just to make sure this wasn't some passing fad like, oh, say, that shaman training he took years before. I think we got him into therapy within the week.

In my heart, I knew it wasn't, but I had to be sure. So I started out with a measured, calm tone, as if he had just told me he preferred vanilla to chocolate (which he does, something I still find strange after twenty-three years of marriage).

"A lot of lesbians feel that way, like they weren't like other girls. Why do you think that means you're a man?"

"I don't know," Jacob would say. "I just think this would explain a lot of things. Maybe if you aren't like other girls and then you come out as a lesbian and suddenly you're like, 'Oh, this all makes sense,' then you're just a lesbian. But if it still doesn't, maybe you're transgender. Maybe I'm transgender. I don't know."

"Okay, we need to get you to a therapist right away. This is a big deal, and you need to talk to someone who knows about this stuff." One of the main things I wanted out of a therapist for him, as well, was someone unbiased, someone he could talk to who didn't have a vested interest in the outcome, because I knew he wouldn't get that from me or our family and friends.

Because we lived in the San Francisco Bay Area at the time, we were lucky enough to have access to some of the best experts on what was then still called gender identity disorder. Kaiser Permanente, our medical provider, sent Jacob to see Dr. Robin Dea, the director of regional mental health for Kaiser Permanente in Northern California, who runs the gender program for the area. She told him something I've seen her repeat countless times in the press since then, and which really resonated—at the time: "Our gender identity is something we feel in our soul. But it is also a continuum, and it evolves."

Of course, the idea that one's gender—which many people feel is a fixed and indelible part of their identity—evolves may sound blasphemous. Especially for gays and lesbians, many of whom believe that the political and social gains the LGBTQ community has achieved over the last few decades have been predicated on mainstream acceptance of sexual orientation as an immutable aspect of one's identity that is fixed at birth.

For Jacob, the idea that our identities can evolve gave him the luxury of embracing his newfound male identity without discounting the previous three decades of his life. He could abandon his lesbian identity without calling it a mistake. As someone who had been actively involved in the lesbian community, he needed to believe that others wouldn't interpret the fact that he was embracing masculinity as an outright rejection of all things female.

Therapy confirmed that Jacob was trans and didn't just want to be a man but indeed *is* a man. As soon as he was sure, and I was sure (perhaps not in that order), I sped the transition along. I know it sounds odd, a lesbian wife rushing her formerly female-identified partner into manhood, but once I was sure Jacob did have gender dysphoria, that this was real, that he was—for lack of a less-educated phrase at this point in our evolution—a man trapped in a woman's body, I wanted to take the next step.

It may be anathema to younger queer and trans folks, many who buck the gender binary and refuse to identify as either a man or a woman—or choose to switch who they are and how they identify on a sometimes-daily basis—but I didn't want to live in limbo. My insistence on remaining within the binary made me feel guilty and old-school, but I was relieved that Jacob never said, "I feel like neither gender" or "I feel like both genders."

If he had, things might be different today. I didn't want to be stuck in the uncomfortable "in between" spot for longer than necessary. Once I identify a problem I want to solve it. Now. Not in a few months. I don't need to ruminate over it or get in touch with my feelings; I just want action. So, as much as it pained me to lose my wife, I very much wanted Jacob to be a man, not someone in between, not something unidentifiable, something hard to explain, and not someone without pronouns that would confound everyone around us (especially our parents, whose reactions I was bracing us both for).

Jacob will probably say I was all aboard the transition train very quickly, and it's true that it seemed like I was. My only way to cope with such a huge change was to embrace this transformation for him.

He was certainly thrilled with my response. But sometimes I would go into the bathroom, turn on the faucet, and cry. I never wanted him to see me look sad or disappointed in his decision to come out and embrace this part of himself.

JACOB (SUZY)

I had no idea Diane had seen this coming. I'd been agonizing over how to tell her, terrified she might leave.

I was so scared. It was almost worse than the first time I came out as lesbian. Then I was a teenager scared my parents would stop loving me. Now I was frightened I might lose the love of my life, the woman I'd spent fifteen years with. Diane was my whole world.

That had been true since the beginning of our relationship. But it was even truer at the point when I was contemplating transition. In the first few years after my back injury, I rarely left the apartment except for doctors' appointments, and she was the only person I see for days at a time. Not to mention by then I was completely dependent upon Diane for my survival.

If we broke up I saw only two options: suicide or moving back in with my parents.

Neither seemed that attractive, and I simply couldn't bear to lose her.

But I also couldn't stand not telling her any longer. I've never been good at keeping things bottled up inside. Sooner or later I have to talk. And something about conversing with Diane has always helped me think. Verbalizing a feeling or an idea and considering her response has helped me know myself better and come to a deeper understanding of where I stand on many topics.

At first I just said the words. I didn't know what I wanted to do with my realization. I wasn't sure I even wanted to transition. I just wanted her to know this was how I was feeling. Maybe saying it would be enough. Maybe identifying as trans was all I'd need. Maybe I wouldn't need to transition.

But for Diane, as she's already mentioned, it's never been enough to just verbalize a problem. She's a solver. Once I said the words she wanted action.

I'm not saying she took over my transition entirely or that she pushed me into anything I didn't already want. But in those early days I was frightened and tentative and might have stretched my transition out over years—especially if she'd asked me to.

But she'd never do that. Instead, she wanted us to move forward. If I was going to become a man, I needed to close the door on Suzy as soon as possible.

Dr. Dea explained the transition process, which is formally guided by The World Professional Association for Transgender Health (WPATH) Standards of Care recommendations. Formerly known as the Harry Benjamin Standards of Care, these recommendations provide a widely accepted protocol for those seeking to make a gender transition.

The Standards recommend a period of "real-life experience," during which the trans person must live and socialize in the garb of their preferred gender. Until quite recently, the candidate for transition had to complete three to twelve months of real-life experience before they could even begin hormone treatment. (As you can probably imagine, this wasn't always easy, or even wise, especially for those transitioning from male to female and unable to pass without the benefits of feminizing surgeries or estrogen treatment).

The current, seventh edition of the Standards of Care dropped the time requirement before approving hormone treatment, yet it still recommends (but no longer requires) twelve to twenty-four months of real-life experience before genital surgery (including hysterectomy).

Dr. Dea had been helping trans patients navigate their transitions for twenty years and by this point used the Standards of Care only as a general guideline. She let her gut guide the details of any particular patient's transition plan.

She encouraged me to immediately begin living as a man, so first I needed a name.

Names are tricky. I'd never liked mine. Susannah "Suzy" Christine Minshall. From birth I'd been called Suzy, and the truth was, to me, "Suzy" wasn't inherently laden with other meanings. It was my name. To me it meant me, with all my own personal traits. And it was the only name Diane had ever called me.

But I'd begun to acknowledge how other people responded to my name, how it seemed to make them look at me differently or make assumptions about the kind of person I was. When I left *Girlfriends* magazine and was no longer working around friends, I decided I needed a work moniker that didn't make me sound like a child, a stripper or a happy homemaker.

The name "Susannah" seemed more restrained and professional, even if my introduction frequently elicited refrains of "Oh, Susannah!"

I wasn't overly fond of either version of my name and often fantasized about changing it to something more gender neutral. But it was my name. Over the years, I had become accustomed to hearing it from those closest to me. And Diane was fond of it—not so much as a name in and of itself, but because it was my name.

By changing my name I risked losing all of that—the connection, the memories, the past associated with it. Choosing to replace it with a new name was deciding to throw away one of the most important gifts my parents had given me. I was desecrating the honor my mother had paid to her favorite sister by naming me after her. While I wanted to find a moniker that suited me, I didn't want to choose something completely at odds with my parents' nomenclature. Different cultures have such different ways of naming their children. Although I could never do it myself as a parent, I loved the parents who let their kids pick their own names, like the famous downhill skier Picabo Street.

Many cultures have naming ceremonies, and in some traditions a person might go through many names in a lifetime. Whenever their name was no longer useful or no longer accurately described the person they'd become, they'd get a new one. In some cultures the child receives a name that describes who he or she is at that moment, while in others, the name is a goal, a challenge, something to strive for. Catholic families like mine often pull their names from Christian saints or figures from the Bible.

When Diane and I were trying to have a baby, we made a list of names we liked. We checked books out of the library and trolled Internet naming sites until we had composed a list inspired by our favorites from Celtic, Native-American, African, and Asian cultures; Hollywood celebrities, fictional characters, and historical figures. We kicked out anything that sounded too "stripperish" or begged to be transformed into a shame-inducing nickname.

With the chances of our *having* a baby diminishing every day, we agreed that robbing the name bank might be our only opportunity to reap the rewards of our research. While some trans people have always *known* their transition name, I didn't. I was open to a lot of options, and the baby-name list seemed like a good place to start, even though many were clearly inappropriate for a grown man. Demonstrating that we're not as unique in our name choosing as we'd like to think, the number of transgender men named Xander proved how popular *Buffy the Vampire Slayer* was with LGBTQ viewers. For someone like me, born decades before those names became popular, taking such a unique moniker would strike people as strange, as though my parents were scarily precognitive.

For similar reasons, Diane nixed two of my favorite names, which had actually both failed to make it on the baby-name list the first time around: one I've never found again but was listed under Native-American names and defined as meaning "that dog over there"—which I've always thought could be a brilliant nickname for some of the men I've met. The other name, WilCe Coyote, started because I'd ask Diane, "what about naming the baby Brentwood?" and she'd reply, "We'll see." She says "we'll see" way too often in real life. Eventually she repeated that phrase enough that I threatened to name the baby "WilCe." But I digress.

My middle name was Christine, and my mom once told me it would have been Christopher had I been born a boy. Although Diane and I considered taking it as my first name, we decided against it, in large part because it's also the name of one of my dad's favorite graduate students. My dad's grad students were the sons my father never had, and there seemed something Freudian about appropriating one of their names. Instead, I kept Christopher as my middle name.

After we kicked out the names that were too young, too hip, or just not me, we decided that embracing my parents' decision to christen me after a saint would help us further narrow our search, and we rejected any name that didn't appear in the Bible or belong to a Catholic saint. We took all those that passed muster, researched their meaning, and found Jacob.

Jacob was supposed to be the first-born but came out second, holding his twin brother's ankle. He later supplanted his brother

Esau. Reading that story, we were struck by the idea of a son who was initially replaced by another child. The person I was meant to be didn't come to the surface for a lifetime. It was an added bonus that Jacob is the patron saint of pilgrims; Christopher is the patron saint of travelers.

❖

Although we researched and processed and went back and forth before choosing my new name, we made our decision rather quickly—within days we had rechristened me Jacob Christopher. And once I had my new name, I transitioned overnight, at least online. After we set up a new e-mail address and I started going by Jacob in the online world, I'd essentially made my debut in the digital world. I started all-new social media sites, changed my e-mail address, took new photos (though I looked very much like I did the day before), but suddenly in the online world, at least, I was now a man.

It's amazing how much we assume about people based on nothing but their name. It reminds me of the times Diane has been attacked for saying she's a woman of color. People have literally insisted she can't be mixed-race because her maiden name is Anderson.

"Anderson isn't a Native-American name," they say. They don't bother to ask questions or imagine reasonable circumstances in which both values could be true; i.e. you could be both mixed-race and have the last name Anderson. For example, your mother might be the person of color in your heritage and she could have married a man named Anderson, or adoption could have played a part in your seemingly incongruent name/race combination. In her case, both of those things are true.

Names certainly can tell you a lot about a person, but they shouldn't automatically do so—especially online.

So, it was a little weird when just changing my name caused other people to treat me differently. People on the phone would respond to me in a new way, once they heard my name—more deferential and often more accommodating. If I sent an e-mail to someone who was a woman, I was treated with more respect; a letter to a man was countered often with jocularity, a sense of sharing, even though I missed many of the signs at first.

In person, other people's reactions to me were even more stunning, especially since it took nearly a year of testosterone injections before my facial hair finally went from a few random strands to something that required shaving. My voice deepened, but never to the point where I couldn't pass as female on the phone. Yet it didn't take long before I was coding as male to strangers, including other men. And when I did, it was like being given entry into a secret society and discovering everything I'd thought about men was only partly true.

DIANE

Jacob and I discussed what it meant to be a man at such great length, and so often, it was clear to everyone—even me—that I was trying to control the process, to control what kind of man Jacob would become. We specifically talked about what kind of man he could be. I recall often using the phrase "Not that kind of man," while pointing at guys on the street, in a magazine, or on the TV screen.

Most of the time Jacob was open to my not-so-subtle attempts to direct him toward becoming a certain type of man. But a few times he put his foot down, like after I explained manscaping (chest waxing and grooming body hair) and told him, "You know, a lot of men shave their legs these days."

He shook his head and laughed. "I don't think so. I'm not going to be that kind of man. Not happening. Sorry."

Eventually it became obvious that I was trying to wrest some kind of control in a situation where I was afraid I had none. Especially after Jacob started testosterone treatments, I worried that runaway masculinity would change him so much I'd lose the person I loved. I feared that his transition would subsume me, making me lose the queer, feminist identity I adored.

Any time I saw a man who was acceptable to me, I pointed him out to Jacob. I was clear that I wanted a metrosexual man, not some absolute paragon of rural masculinity. I'd left those guys behind in my hometown and wasn't nostalgic for that part of Idaho. When I saw men dressed in fleece and flannel or sporting hairy backs, hideous beer bellies, or worse, socks with sandals, I'd nudge Jacob, point out the unacceptable representation, and say, "Not that." The phrase "Not that" became common shorthand in our household.

I did this so often during the first three months of Jacob's transition that one time, in a moment of pure exasperation with my insistence on what kind of man he could or could not be, Jacob exclaimed, in the middle of a department store, "Then what kind of man *can* I be?"

I thought for a minute or two and blurted out, "Ryan Seacrest."

I'm not exactly sure why the *American Idol* host seemed such the perfect model for acceptable masculinity, but he's a decent-looking guy, and I'd always admired his ambiguous metrosexuality. He seems like the kind of man who's comfortable in his masculinity and doesn't need to prove it. He's blond and clean-shaven, urban and urbane, polite yet driven, non-threatening, and I can imagine his chest is completely hairless. I could envision Ryan Seacrest getting a facial and sporting designer duds more than I could imagine him chopping wood and building fences (ironically, two things Jacob had already done for years).

Jacob paused, then said resolutely, "Okay."

He sounded relieved. Seacrest was a model of masculinity and physical role model we could both agree on. He was macho light—no testosterone overdose there.

Ryan Seacrest begat a new mantra for me, "What Would Ryan Do?" After that, whenever I bought Jacob new clothes—which I did often in those early days; after all, we had to replace a whole wardrobe and I deserved the retail therapy—I'd hold the shirt or pants up on the hanger and ask myself, "What would Ryan do?"

If Seacrest would wear it, I bought it; if not, I passed. I used the Seacrest model on everything from messenger bags to hair gel.

I've always felt, as Jacob's co-pilot in life, that it was my job to push him to be the best he could be and to make himself happy. If he says he wants to do a graphic novel, the next day I buy him ink and drawing pads. If he says he really loves V-neck tees all of a sudden, I buy him five in a rainbow of colors. I've always wanted to be responsive to him, perhaps the way everyone wants someone to be responsive to them.

So while his transition was deeply personal for both of us, for me it was also another project at which to excel. I wanted it to be the best transition anyone could have. That's what a good wife does, right?

JACOB (SUZY)

It'd been nearly twenty years since I came out as a lesbian, but in some ways, my transition to male was a lot like my transition to lesbian. I say transition to lesbian, because once I started to meet other lesbians, a funny thing happened. I started to change.

I cut my hair shorter. I started listening to the music my new friends introduced me to: Cris Williamson, Meg Christian, Ferron, Tret Fure, Joan Armatrading, Diedre McCalla. I started wearing butchier clothes and reading books by and about lesbians.

In other words, I'd discovered that while being a lesbian was a sexual orientation, it was also much more. A whole lesbian community, a lesbian culture, existed, and I'd started the process of acculturation.

The same thing happened when I came out as trans. And, surprisingly, it didn't look a lot different from my acculturation to lesbianism.

I cut off my hair, I started wearing men's clothes, I started reading books by and about trans people, and I began listening to music by trans musicians like Katastrophe, Joshua Klipp, Shawna Virago, Athens Boys Choir, and Lipstick Conspiracy.

I also began binding my breasts, a painful and tedious process necessary for anyone with breasts to pass as male while waiting for chest surgery. Getting top surgery requires passing certain milestones in your medical transition and the ability to shell out five to ten thousand dollars. If you're pinched for money, because all your spare change is in a jar marked "top surgery," you wrap drugstore Ace bandages around your chest until your breasts are flattened enough that under a T-shirt (or two) other people can't tell you have a female anatomy. A lot of FTMs have to bind this way, despite the risks: the long-term pressure can actually damage breast tissue so much it impedes top surgery. Ace bandages are much worse than binders.

I was remarkably privileged. I had to use elastic bandages for only a few weeks before Diane bought me a binder, which is a garment that stretches from just above your waist to under your arms. People have used it as a post-surgery garment for years as well, so it's readily available. Nowadays there are websites and Listservs for trans men where guys trade things like binders and share tips on passing as male. Binders let most guys pass almost immediately. And when you're trans, passing in public becomes a critical issue, one that affects your mental health, your safety, and even the speed at which you can transition.

Because I was at home instead of going into an office, I didn't have to wear the binder ten hours a day, every weekday, as some men do. And taking a settlement on my worker's comp case soon funded my top surgery, ending my need for a binder altogether, and I passed mine on. Still, I know other trans guys who haven't been as fortunate and have instead worn their binders for years, even a decade, while trying to save enough money for top surgery.

But, like me, they loved the look of a flat chest, and passing made the discomfort bearable. Fortunately, packing was far less painful.

As a trans guy, whether or not you are going to have your genitals altered with gender-reassignment surgery (colloquially known as bottom surgery), many of us feel more comfortable with a bulge in our pants. Sure, it helps us pass not to look like a mannequin in jeans, but there's also something psychologically fulfilling about having a particular heft in one's briefs. And it's even better if your junk—be it flesh, silicon, or cotton—can pass the feel test. If someone gropes you in a bar, the last thing you want is for the groper to sense there is anything different between your package and the next.

If God hasn't blessed you with twig and berries, you can find a few ways to create the look and feel of the real thing. One is a tried-and-true method that has worked for teenage boys the world over: stuff a sock or one side of a pair of nylons full of other socks and just cram the bundle in your underwear.

But most trans guys opt for something a little more technical: a silicone packer that mimics the natural form and feel of a bio guy's pork and beans. (Of course if you prefer, you can also get something that looks like a dolphin, but most trans guys are seeking a modicum of realism.) You can also get a packer that has been modified to allow you to pee standing up. Often called a piss-n-packer it is typically a silicon packer with a hole drilled through the center. A tube is threaded through the shaft of the packer and extends a couple of inches so it can be maneuvered up to the urethral opening. At the top of the tube is a small reservoir (usually the top of a liquid medicine dispenser), which captures the urine and directs it through the head of the packer.

Standing to pee uses different muscles than sitting. You usually have to surreptitiously hold the piss-n-packer against the body with one hand, and trying to slow the flow of urine so it doesn't overflow the tiny teaspoon-sized reservoir takes some real discipline, so it's wise to practice using it in a shower. That's what I did. Otherwise your first live test run may see you pee your pants—and end up with a hand full of urine—in a public restroom.

Another piece of beneficial equipment is a harness, because the most embarrassing thing is for your package—sock or silicone—to drop out your pants' leg and land on the locker room floor.

With my body and its modifications under control, I continued my enculturalization into the trans community. I started gravitating toward people who'd gone through parallel issues, becoming virtual friends with Helen Boyd, who wrote the book *My Husband Betty* after her spouse came out as a cross-dresser (and later as a trans woman). Helen was going through a bit of what Diane was but in reverse; she was being now perceived as a lesbian and Diane was being perceived as straight. Neither was particularly true.

We bonded over being feminists who had found ourselves suddenly part of communities that didn't exactly seem eager to embrace feminist tenets; and we were both discouraged by that. Helen was taking a proactive approach to educating cross-dressers (and sometimes their conservative wives) about the insights feminism had to offer. I was mostly just complaining about the number of times I heard a trans guy say something sexist.

Stuck at home I came to rely on my virtual friendships, and they helped me learn more about trans issues than I ever could have on my own (even with Google). I wanted to understand trans politics, trans history, trans art, trans music, and get to know the diversity of the trans community. I wanted to immerse myself in the trans culture, to become a part of it as I had with gay and lesbian culture. So I read nearly every book I could find written by an out trans person. I reached out to trans leaders, authors, artists, and journalists. Soon my conversations became the basis for a weekly syndicated column, TransNation. Printed in LGBTQ publications across the country, TransNation profiled a different trans or gender-variant person each week and, in doing so, exposed readers to the colorful individuals that populate the surprisingly diverse trans community.

But when I'd started seeing Dr. Dea, I wouldn't have imagined I'd write a column or end up speaking with hundreds of trans folk. Back then I was still out of work, and although I was taking classes they were all online. This relative isolation limited any real-world sort of test to my walking around my neighborhood dressed in my new persona.

We were living in a great Foster City apartment complex with a little pond in the courtyard and a park nearby. When I went out walking, as I did several times a day with our rescue dog, Skippy, his notable Chihuahua-Schipperke presence commanded the attention of those we met. (Something about Skippy's appearance as a perfect miniaturization of classic dog looks really appealed to men. Honestly, from the first day we drove an hour to pick him up at an out-of-town shelter, random men had approached me to say, "Great dog!")

I remember being really excited one day when I ran into someone I didn't know—and I *passed*. So did Skippy. We were coming home from our afternoon walk when a Latino man approached me about introducing Skippy to his Chihuahua.

At first I thought he just wanted to set up a play date, which isn't uncommon for pet owners in our area. And he did, sort of. He wanted to engage Skippy's stud services, and the conversation we had around said transaction proved to me that the man thought he was talking to another guy. It's hard to pinpoint how, but the way he talked about women, even female dogs, made it clear he wasn't seeing me as one of them.

Skippy had already had surgery that made him less of a man (in the eyes of the world), and I hadn't yet had surgery that would make me more of one. But we had both passed. The guy didn't realize that neither of us had testicles at the time. For a brief moment we weren't perceived as a lesbian and her neutered pet. We were men. Real, virile men.

My first experience as just another guy thrilled me. I wanted more. I was on my way to becoming Jacob.

CHAPTER FOUR

OUR PROFESSIONAL IDENTITIES

JACOB (SUZY)

For a lot of trans folk, transitioning on the job is the hardest part of their transformation. First of all, it's difficult for people who knew you as Susannah to immediately start calling you Jacob, especially when nothing else about you has changed. So if you not only remain with the same employer but also transition in place, rather than taking off time and returning as another person, it can be awkward. Life would be much simpler if you could be whisked away to an exotic locale, undergo a complete overhaul, and return an entirely new person. Back in the 1950s and '60s, people like Christine Jorgensen would take a holiday to Sweden or Copenhagen. Now places like Thailand and parts of South America offer the perfect getaways for a tan and penis tuck. But these days, most trans folks not only transition in place; they undergo their physical transformation in front of an audience one day at a time.

You know that old saying about no one wanting to see how sausage is made? And I bet a butterfly isn't as gorgeous when you can watch its miraculous transformation through Plexiglas. Transitioning is a little like that. The middle ground is awkward and often unattractive. You go through all the ungainly and embarrassing elements of puberty, but you get to experience them while trying to maintain your adult world. As a teen, your friends were experiencing the same changes, so you weren't the only one with a zit-covered face or strange appearances of hair in unexpected places, or your raging hormones or wildly vacillating emotions.

Comparatively, I had it easy. I wasn't working full time. I was freelancing for *Bitch* magazine, which mostly involved writing book reviews. I worked from home. As I mentioned earlier, my transition at work consisted of me sending my *Bitch* editor an e-mail saying I'd come out as trans and would be transitioning. She'd responded with congratulations and offered to change my name on the book review I'd just submitted.

That was it. I'd transitioned professionally.

At the time I was wrapping a longer piece, which was a critique of fat-phobia on reality shows like *The Biggest Loser* and *Celebrity Fit Club*. I had already completed most of my interviews with a number of feminist authors and academics for the piece, but I needed to wrap up a few things a few weeks after I changed my name. Things had been going so well I didn't even think about how the name change might impact the responses. Suddenly one of the women who'd been interested in the story lost her enthusiasm. And I sparked the ire of another, a feminist scholar, who took me to task for addressing her as Ms. in the e-mail, "such a gendered term," she complained, instead of Dr., which she would have preferred.

She also accused me of "invading" her "intellectual backyard," which confused me. The best I could figure, she thought I intended to take credit for her ideas rather than quoting her. That's something a stereotypical man might do, so maybe I can't fault her for seeing "Jacob" and responding accordingly.

But she went on to question why I was even writing for a publication like *Bitch*. Worse, her criticism made me question myself. Overnight I'd become an outsider in the feminist world. I felt like an unwanted intruder. I asked my editors if they still wanted me to write for them. There weren't a lot of male bylines in the publication. Maybe that was by design.

Bitch soon reassured me that I would always be a welcome contributor. My piece, "Who's the Biggest Loser," was not only published in *Bitch* but picked up by several other outlets, including AlterNet.

(Until recently—when I raised the ire of numerous trans women in an online opinion piece that elicited charges of "mansplaining" and other sexist crimes, this initial interaction with the doctorate-holding academic was the closest I've come to *Testosterone Files* author Max Wolf Valerio's experience while transitioning from a radical feminist and contributor to the quintessential women-of-color anthology, *This Bridge Called My Back*, to a trans man accused of being sexist.)

Not long after I came out, I started working with *LiP* magazine, editing their film section from home. I was introduced to the freelance writers I'd be working with simply as Jacob, the new film editor.

Many of the writers were men, but they accepted my management and editing in a way that guys hadn't, not even when I was the acting supervisor of a maintenance staff. Maybe this experience was different because I was supervising white-collar vs. blue-collar guys. But I think my name and their assumptions based on that name made the difference.

In women's eyes, it seemed, going from Suzy to Jacob had transformed me from ally to outsider. For men I'd gone from outsider to respected colleague. It was a strange transition. And it was just beginning.

DIANE

By the time Jacob realized he was a man, I had made a name for myself in LGBTQ publishing. The two of us, along with Heather Findlay and Bonnie Simon, had launched a lesbian magazine in the early 1990s called *Girlfriends*, and even though I was run out of the company seven years later, I honestly thought that time of my life would be my professional peak. I was already an executive editor in my twenties, was interviewing celebrities and hanging out with (minor) rock stars, and was helping bring lesbian issues to the national stage. After reporters from *Elle*, *The New York Times*, and *Playboy* interviewed me, I thought I would never top that experience. After *Girlfriends* came my own magazine, *Alice*, which landed me a ton of consulting and freelancing gigs for both LGBTQ and mainstream magazines and websites. And then *Curve* magazine came calling.

I can honestly say that working at *Curve* was in the top two or three experiences of my lifetime. When I first came on board, I wasn't sure how well I'd do or how well I'd get along with the staff, but I fell into it like I'd been doing it my whole life. Frances "Franco" Stevens, the publisher, had been injured not long before I got there and had been undergoing different therapies to treat the damage to her foot, so she couldn't walk on it. I'd been afraid to let any employer know I'd been diagnosed with fibromyalgia in 2004.

I'd undergone a year of testing to find out why, once again, I was in so much pain and was so exhausted. When my doctor first mentioned fibromyalgia, she asked me to promise not to go look it up on the Internet that night, to wait until I really knew I had it. I did, and I now understand why she asked that of me, because on the web, tons of blogs and Listserve support groups of people have them talking about how fibro has disabled them. The stories are terrifying, especially since most people on the fibro boards have lost their jobs due to disability. Losing my career was tantamount to death back then, and both terrified me.

Fibromyalgia is a nervous-system disorder characterized by chronic widespread pain, and it comes with a whole host of other problems like joint pain, irritable bowel/bladder syndromes, depression, extreme fatigue, and what many call fibro fog—a sort of cognitive disorder in which you literally can't think straight, can't remember things, can't think things through like you normally would.

When I started at *Curve*, I didn't mention the diagnosis and probably didn't mention it the whole first year, but Franco had set a standard for showing that people with disabilities didn't need to be forced out of the workforce, and over time I would open up to my coworkers about the fibro. Occasionally I needed to work from home, but more often than not I was putting in work above and beyond the call of duty.

Girlfriends was my baby and I always wanted to see it do well, but once I joined *Curve, Girlfriends* became my main competitor. I thought there was a place at the table for both of us (after all, there's an adage that you have to have strong competitors to be a strong magazine; if there's only one magazine in your niche you're lost on the newsstand). But it was a competition at the newsstand and I reveled in each win, usually in the form of which celebrity I managed to wrangle for our cover. I rushed to tell the media about each score. I put out a better magazine in part because Franco gave me the freedom to do so. Fighting with my old business partner for readership was strangely validating for me, because in a way I felt like it was saying to her that if she had just let me stay, just let me continue on their team, they'd be whooping *Curve*'s ass right now.

In my seven years at *Curve* I learned to be the nice girl; Franco used to always say, "We're the nice ones," which was meant to serve as a reminder of why we didn't trash talk other gay or lesbian magazines and why we tried to do everything ethically sound. At first I thought it was weirdly uncompetitive, especially coming from an ex-boxer, but then I realized that it was Franco saying, you can fight a clean fight and still win. And that's what I did, especially as I moved into the role of editor in chief at *Curve*. It was the first time anyone besides Franco had held that title, and I held it and her in such high regard that I never wanted to lose it.

After several issues where we clearly trounced *Girlfriends* on the newsstand (a look at the covers from their last two years of publication show that they were creatively flailing), we received paperwork at the office: Heather or, rather, HAF Enterprises was suing us. Here we go again, I thought. Heather had alleged that we hired a former employee of hers (which we did) and that he stole business contacts and bad-mouthed her to former advertisers.

I was named in the suit and had to give testimony and watch as it stretched on so long that that employee literally had a nervous breakdown and left the company. Franco and the board of directors worried about whether this lawsuit would take us to the brink, like the first one did when Catherine Deneuve sued the company to force a legal name change of the magazine, which was originally called *Deneuve*. That first lawsuit cost tens of thousands of dollars and drove the company to near bankruptcy; Suze Orman, then a friend of the company, suggested they just fold. But Franco persevered and so did the magazine.

But with Heather's lawsuit, it was an endless mess and one that I wasn't legally allowed to talk about. Friends from the old company would call and ask how things were, and I wanted desperately to tell them that HAF was up to its old tricks. Eventually the lawsuit was settled and we took a big financial hit, but we didn't close shop as *Girlfriends* did not long after. Seeing it fade away was sad for me. My baby was dead and its place in lesbian history still unwritten, but I felt glad that I stayed ethical and nice throughout that battle.

I loved *Curve* for so many reasons: the intellectual freedom to create, to speak directly to the readers without a filter, the feeling of so much female energy and personal power. And I loved the team that had developed around me. My managing editor Katie Peoples, production manager Ondine Kilker, art director Stefanie Liang, operations manager Flo Enriquez, ad director Diana Berry, and so many others became close personal friends, but none more than my associate editor Rachel Shatto. I recognized Rachel's brilliance the first year she came in as an intern.

I took pride in my intern program at *Curve*, and it was really tailored to groom young writer/editors to move into staff positions if and when they opened up. During my eight years there, many of the junior editors in both art and edit departments had come through the intern program. Many of my interns at *Girlfriends*, after seeing nothing but chaos and struggle, left publishing altogether. But not at *Curve*. Many women who were interns or junior editors from my time, like Amy Silverman (now photo editor at *Outside* magazine), Julia Bloch (now an award-winning poet), and Jocelyn Voo (a social-media strategist for *Fortune 100* brands) stayed in or near the field and are still making great strides today.

Rachel Shatto is too. It doesn't surprise me at all. The month she was hired I narcissistically dubbed her mini-me for her ability to recognize the same social trends and story leads and her writing style so similar to mine. I told her that first month that I saw her running the magazine someday. Today, she's the managing editor at *Curve*.

❖

With my deep love of my work at *Curve*, my relationship with its women (those who created the magazine and those who read it), and whatever role I had in the national lesbian landscape, Jacob's transition gave both of us a bit of a panic over what it might mean for me and my career. I was a fairly well-known queer woman, so I met with Franco and tearfully asked if she foresaw a problem with my remaining the editor in chief of the world's largest lesbian magazine.

I offered to keep the change under wraps and essentially enter the closet. She told me she accepted both of us and that my right to be at the helm of *Curve* was unchanged in her mind. What a relief.

In fact, she invited Jacob to blog about his transition experience for *Curve*—which he did. By this point Jacob and I had gotten our first Blind Eye mystery novel accepted by the publishing house Bold Strokes Books. A solely lesbian book publisher at the time, the company has since expanded to include a whole gay-male imprint, a youth imprint, and works by bisexual and trans authors. But at the time it hadn't yet published a man.

We asked if Jacob should use a pen name or keep his name off the book altogether. Thankfully, Len Barot, our publisher, said no.

She wasn't sure how female readers would respond to our names—would they mistake us for a straight couple and dismiss us as not being LGBTQ?—but she was willing, perhaps even eager, to find out. She strongly believed her readers were ready to stretch their comfort zones and accept a trans guy writing lesbian content.

That amazed us, because that was exactly what Jacob and I wanted to continue to write. We chose to write lesbian and queer characters because not only we had lived in that world up to that point, but we wanted to continue be a part of it.

Moreover, Len didn't want Jacob, as a new novelist, to begin his literary life in a closet. We've now written three Blind Eye mysteries together. While we still wonder if having a male and female with a shared last name on the book jacket reduces sales, our true fans have never complained. All they need to do is read our bios to know our story and how we remain grounded in the queer community.

But even with this kind of uniform support in our professional world, I wasn't doing as well with things as my outward presentation might have led people to think.

JACOB (SUZY)

One night, not long after I officially came out to Diane, I woke to find her sobbing. It was the middle of the night.

"What's wrong?" I asked.

"You're so pretty," she cried. "It's not fair. You have everything I always wanted, and you don't want it."

Diane grew up being jealous of the skinny, blond, blue-eyed girls she admired. It's part of why she liked having me on her arm and why she liked to dress me up in the clothes she couldn't wear. Somehow having me around kept her closer to a physical appearance she wished she had.

I would come to realize, in the process of my transition, that no matter how much you dislike some part of yourself, someone else out there in the world is probably desperate to have it.

It became even clearer to me later, when I found out a friend from my ranger days had just been diagnosed with breast cancer, how much someone else can be desperate to have some part of yourself that you dislike. My friend was terrified she was going to lose a breast. Then she learned she had to have a double mastectomy.

At the time she was battling to keep her breasts, I was voluntarily *choosing* to remove mine. I was considering chest reconstruction, which would remove healthy breast tissue, and I so wished I could give mine to her.

Wouldn't it be great if we could have a body-parts swap meet where trans boys and girls could exchange the parts they didn't want for those they did? Everyone would come out winners, with authentic, 100-percent natural organs, genitalia, musculature, and vocal chords.

I was reminded, too, that so many of us dislike our bodies. It's hardly the sole domain of trans folk. Take even the most gorgeous women in Hollywood, and chances are they don't like something about themselves.

DIANE

My internal struggle with Jacob's transition slipped out in the oddest places and was evidenced by the fact that for the first three months—or maybe the first *six*—I felt compelled to over-explain my situation to complete strangers.

I was having to confront how Jacob's transition impacted my own identity, and instead of talking it out with the people I cared most about, I found myself expressing it in absurd ways to service workers.

If I was at the grocery store and a clerk complimented my handbag, I'd say, "Thanks. My husband gave that to me. Except he used to be a woman. He used to be my wife. He had a sex change. But I'm still a lesbian."

The reply stunned nearly everyone, especially the clerks at the grocery store who heard it numerous times and rarely had an easy time with an appropriate response. How exactly is one supposed to respond to that? But this type of absurd blathering on about my identity, past and present, went on for a long time.

I introduced Jacob as "my husband who used to be my wife" for several months. I told everyone I encountered that my wife was now a man, but I was still a lesbian. It had officially become my turn to "protest too much."

I worried about the junior editors and other employees below me, as well as my freelancer writers and my overall lesbian community.

But I was also gaining strength and confidence. Often when women would question me in those early days, asking how I could be a lesbian with a husband, I would ask them, "Is your identity tied to your partner's genitals?" They'd invariably say no and my fight would be won.

I honestly didn't think my identity needed to change just because his did.

I remember very early when we lived in San Francisco that I tried to claim a bisexual identity. It went over so poorly I never did it again. I used the words *queer* and *lesbian* interchangeably, but by that point, I'd been with women for more than twenty years, and my cultural landscape, my interests, and my identifications were with other queer women. I wasn't planning to change my identity as a lesbian simply because my partner's gender identity had changed.

CHAPTER FIVE

CHEST SURGERY

JACOB (SUZY)

In October 2005, we reached a settlement with workers' comp. Diane was adamant that we earmark some of the money for my top surgery. At the time I resisted. We needed money for so many other things: medical bills and deferred purchases.

But Diane insisted. And I can't express how grateful I am that she did.

At the time no insurance covered the "elective" surgery, and trans men often had to scrimp and save for a decade before they could afford to pay for it themselves. (It's not surprising that so many have turned to fund-raising parties and other creative avenues to make the money.) The settlement and Diane's insistence saved me from a similar fate.

When I told my mom that I'd scheduled chest surgery, she told me she was afraid Diane would leave me.

"She's a lesbian," Mom said. "It's her job." She was referring to Diane's professional lesbianism as editor in chief of *Curve*. "Don't you think you should slow down? Don't you think you should wait?"

"*Wait*? For what?" Diane asked, when I repeated the conversation.

I think my mom was still hoping if I waited long enough I'd change my mind.

"I'm transitioning," I told my mom. "This isn't something I'm thinking about. It's something I'm *doing*. I'm taking testosterone. My body's changing."

I wanted to yell, "THIS IS REALLY HAPPENING." But I didn't. When she'd seen me the previous Christmas I was a girl with shoulder-length hair. She couldn't believe that ten months later I wouldn't even have breasts.

My mom told me that a friend of hers said it was just awful that I was planning to go through all this pain and surgery and expense, just because I didn't like my body. *Nobody* likes their body, she'd said.

To a certain degree, she's right. Not very many people like their bodies. But the relationship trans people have with their bodies is far more complex. Even then I'd read enough to know that no amount of surgery would give me some perfect male body. While plastic surgeons have honed the skill of breast reconstruction and transforming penile structures into a passable vagina, they have been far less competent in creating a respectable penis.

Maybe it stems from the fact that most surgeons are men. Maybe they inherently assume their own anatomy cannot be approximated while a woman's can be tinkered with and even improved upon with their intervention.

Or maybe, as a generation of surgeons who performed often unwanted surgery upon intersex children crudely put it, it really is "easier to create a hole than a pole."

Either way, surgeons have done a better job giving transgender women the complete package, an entirely gender congruent body. You can't look at someone like actress Candis Cayne and not think, damn that's a beautiful woman. Genetics helped in her case, but plastic surgery did part of the job too.

Still, no matter how much money a trans person has to spend on multiple surgeries, the body they end up with will always be a pale reflection of what their body could have been if they'd been born in a body reflecting the sex they self-identify with. Man-made bodies simply aren't as well-crafted as nature-made ones, and they often require a lot of work that nobody knows about (Google "transgender vaginal dilator" for one example), even after surgery. But my mom's friend is also right. Many, many of us have issues with our bodies. In that, trans people aren't alone. It's a matter of degree. As much as most people don't like their extra weight or the way their nose looks or whatever, most people don't feel so out of sorts with their body that they'll go to any lengths to change it. But many trans people would. I've read many stories of trans girls who tried to cut off their penises so they could be girls in real life.

The rate of suicide attempts is three times the national average for transgender people, and part of that has to do with not being able to easily have bodies that are congruent with our gender identities. In the trans community we call what I had chest surgery or chest-masculinization surgery; my doctor called it a keyhole incision bilateral mastectomy. I chose this surgery because I had small breasts (with breasts over a size B cup a different surgery is usually recommended), and I wanted to retain sensation in my nipples.

My surgeon (who has since retired) made an incision around each areola and basically removed breast tissue with a scalpel (sometimes it's done through liposuction as well), contouring it a bit so it replicates a man's chest. My areolas were cut down to the size of a nickel, again because men's areolas are much smaller than women's. I now have scars that are maybe a couple of inches each way jutting out from my nipples.

I wanted this surgery mainly because breasts are one of those things that signify femaleness the most. I wanted to remove what was causing my incongruent sense of self. Breasts code female. It's difficult to have breasts and pass as male. And when I imagined my body, I didn't see breasts.

Still, I admit, as I faced the surgery I wondered if I was doing the right thing. I love queer theory and the theoretical arguments that the separations we make between genders, or natural and machine or man and monster, are all arbitrary and difficult to pin down, wispy smoke-like aberrations that our cultural linguistics and enforced behavior construct.

But in some ways I'll always be influenced by my heritage. After all, I was raised in a conservative area of rural Idaho by Christian ecologists. And a small part of me wondered what I was doing by remaking myself into what one trans artist calls the new-millennium cyborg. It seemed like such a huge step to take from farm boy to cyborg.

Ironically, I'd previously tended to defend the status quo, believing that people should leave bodies pretty much as the creative forces made them. In college I told one friend I wouldn't stay friends with her if she got a nose job. And when my parents briefly considered plastic surgery to alter my sister Jennye's telltale Down syndrome features, I was quite simply *appalled*.

That was the same sentiment I had years later, when I was living in Northampton and heard about a lesbian who'd decided to have her breasts removed. I couldn't believe a doctor would do that. I couldn't believe someone could just say, "I don't like this totally healthy part of myself," and a surgeon would agree to cut it off. Now I was that person.

I'm totally aware of the deep hypocrisy inherent in my transitioning. Testosterone and surgeries have altered my facial features and significantly changed my body. I no longer believe things I believed twenty years ago. It seems like any time I make small-minded proclamations about what's right and wrong, it's only a matter of time until I find myself on the opposite side of my proclaimed divide. A trickster spirit seems to stalk me, tricking me into stumbling backward into the most significant lessons of my life.

If I'm vehemently opposed to something, I'll almost always end up walking in those shoes, doing the thing that appalled me or accepting the belief I criticized. Then I forget about making those kinds of absolute statements and walk into another teaching moment.

Here I was ready to surgically alter my body for aesthetic reasons. Or maybe it wasn't aesthetic. Maybe it really was more like the removal of a diseased organ or medically necessary surgery—a necessary action to make me well.

The night before my chest surgery, Diane and I had one of our worst fights ever. It was a jumble of fears, blame-throwing, anxiety, and terror of the unknown beast I'd unleashed into the once safe and still forest of our relationship.

She was afraid I might not wake up from surgery. She was afraid I'd abandon her.

I was afraid my mom was right. I was afraid Diane would leave me. I was afraid no one would ever love me for what I was about to become.

DIANE

I sat alone in our car, parked in a lot outside of a surgical center, sobbing. The kind of sobbing that engulfs your whole body, the kind of uncontrollable reaction to grief that just envelopes you, has you lunging forward with despair as you cry out. So much snot was running down my face I didn't see any point in even bothering to wipe it away.

Suzy was inside. She'd just been taken back into the surgery room after the hospital had made me sign my life away.

Or, rather, they'd made me sign Suzy's life away. The statement they handed me said I understood this surgery could be fatal, that she might never wake up after the operation, that the moment I last saw her, hooked up to tubes and being wheeled past me on a hospital cot, could be my last image of her. That could have been our last moment together.

I was terrified I was about to lose her. Even if death didn't steal her from me, I was afraid Suzy would never walk out of that hospital. This was the moment it *really* hit me that *she* was already gone.

I couldn't help but think about another time I was outside a hospital while the person I loved went under the knife.

My first wife, Tina, had found a lump in her breast when we were both just nineteen or twenty. She went in for a simple biopsy. Then a nurse came out and asked if she could speak with me. Something else had come to their attention, something more critical than a lump. Something so severe Tina had been immediately taken in for emergency surgery.

They'd discovered she had Crohn's disease and an intestinal blockage that could kill her. They'd rushed Tina into surgery and removed several feet of her intestines. When they let me back in the room to see her, her neck and chest were still covered in swaths of dried blood. I fought back tears.

She stayed in the hospital a week recovering. Every day for seven days I came in as soon as visiting hours started and sat beside her bed until visiting hours ended.

Mostly I just talked to her, about everything from the need for prison reform to what the environmental movement was up in arms about now, why President Bush Senior was an idiot for calling out Roseanne Barr (about what I don't even recall), and how great it was that 2Live Crew had sold two million copies of their new album.

Every night, I'd go home and cry hysterically. I cried out of loneliness. I sobbed about losing her. And every night I wrote in my journal about how much I loved Tina, how we were going to survive this and spend the rest of our lives together.

The biopsy came back negative. The lump didn't indicate breast cancer. Yet I lost her anyway. We were divorced within a year. I could trace our end back to that week in the hospital. After that surgery Tina was never the same.

I hadn't been the only one who'd seen death skulking around the halls of the hospital. The surgery had given Tina a glimpse of her mortality. Suddenly, she felt like she could die at any moment. Suddenly she began to think of all the experiences she hadn't yet had. She thought about how she'd never really sowed her wild oats. She started living fast, as though she were trying to cram years of living into a few mere months. She acted as though death were always just a step behind her and could catch up with her at any moment.

Even though the surgeons hadn't given Tina Crohn's disease, it was hard not to blame them for taking her away from me, for planting the seeds of our demise.

But at least, when I lost Tina I'd gotten a hell of a consolation prize. I'd gotten Suzy.

And we'd had fifteen glorious years together. (By the way, Tina is happy and healthy now, still beautiful and living in Idaho with her wife of many years.)

But now I was back at the mercy of a surgeon, whose scalpel would surely steal Suzy away from me. I couldn't imagine what my life would be like without her. So I was sobbing.

Even if someone had been there with me, I don't think they could've consoled me. I didn't care who could hear or what they might have thought. At that moment I was grieving for the woman I'd loved for fifteen years. For all the dreams that we would never fulfill together, the loss of the future I'd imagined with her. I sobbed because I was afraid the life I'd imagined where we would grow old together and die together two old women holding hands would never come to pass.

A few months before the surgery, Suzy and I had gone to New Orleans, which had always been our special place.

I'd fallen in love with it during my first visit, when I was fifteen and my Aunt Luanne took me to the World's Fair. New Orleans had been a feast for my budding sensations. I'd fallen in love the first time I glimpsed the gritty Bourbon Street and unbridled sexuality of the French Quarter. I'd fallen in love with the slow muddy river that embraced the city, the smell of gardenias that seemed to permeate the uptown district.

After I graduated from high school in Payette, Idaho, I immediately hit the road and moved to New Orleans. I went to college there, first at Tulane, then Xavier. I moved back and forth between Idaho and New Orleans several times. I could never seem to make a living in the city, but I also couldn't seem to stay away. And ever since that first visit I'd dragged nearly every person I'd ever loved to the city.

In our first year together I'd introduced Suzy to New Orleans, sharing with her all the things I loved the most about it. Even though she was uncomfortable at first, like a fish out of water, I could see her starting to fall in love too, which just made me love her more. An appreciation of all things New Orleans—the food, the neighborhoods, the music, the multicultural residents—was one of the values we shared and one of the things we bonded over.

On that last trip to the city I loved, I remember feeling like Suzy and I were on the precipice of something. Something big seemed like it was on the horizon. But I couldn't put my finger on it at the time. I couldn't understand what it was.

When Christopher Columbus landed in America they say the First Peoples didn't see the ships coming. They had no concept of ships. Maybe they saw something out in the horizon, something ominous and dark, but they had no way to know what was coming.

It was quite literally, unprecedented. That was how I'd felt in New Orleans—like something was out there, something was coming, but I couldn't even fathom what it might be.

All the snapshots from that trip showed me beaming, my hair plastered on my face from the sweat and humidity, slightly drunk and gluttonous and alive. In all her photos, Suzy too was smiling, and in her crop top and tight capris (the most feminine outfit she'd probably ever worn as an adult) she looked every inch the model I'd always thought she could have been.

But now, if I looked closely, I'd have to admit a shadow might be lurking there, something behind her eyes that hinted of something hidden there, a secret or a long-dormant desire, an unfulfilled destiny. At the time neither of us had a name for what was there.

But now, in the hospital parking lot, the horizon had reached me, the future, was now. Suzy was in the process of becoming

Jacob. And as much as I'd pushed her to get here, I was nearly sick with grief at all I was losing.

It was so ironic that embracing her dreams was crushing my own.

Still, I thought, we would get through this.

I shivered. I'd had the same thought while waiting for Tina to get out of surgery. What was different this time?

I set my jaw. What was different? I was. I was no longer a twenty-year-old but was in my late thirties. I'd locked it in with Suzy when I was a hot young woman. I couldn't start over again now, even if I was willing to. I couldn't afford to lose this time. This time no consolation prize was waiting in the wings. This time I was resolute.

I would not let this be the end of us. If I had to, I'd wrestle fate itself to do my bidding. I refused to let our story end this way. I refused to lose our relationship, even if that meant letting Suzy go and embracing Jacob instead.

I was certain I'd love Suzy regardless of what form she took, what name she responded to, what pronoun she preferred. Her essence would remain, even if, from my perspective, it were as though a beautiful butterfly had flown into the cocoon of the surgery center and would emerge a caterpillar.

I forced myself to stop crying. I wiped away my tears. I blew my nose. I reapplied my lipstick. Then I marched back into the surgery center, ready to meet my husband.

JACOB (SUZY)

While I was recovering from chest surgery I read Tania Katan's cancer memoir, *My One-Night Stand with Cancer*, to write a review for *Bitch*. It felt sacrilegious.

I was pretty sure I was going to hell anyway because I'd exaggerated my likelihood of having breast cancer when I was trying to get my insurance to cover my required mammogram. The company had denied my request anyway, because, at thirty-eight, I was considered "too young" for breast cancer.

That's what Katan had been told too, when she was twenty-one and found a lump in her breast. But the cancer didn't care how old she was, and it took one of her breasts. Then it came back ten years later and took the other.

I made a big scene about the insurance denial, bemoaning how I could end up like my brilliant thirty-five-year-old violinist cousin who'd died suddenly the previous year—even though her cancer wasn't in her breast tissue and a mammogram wouldn't have saved her life. I played on a nurse's heartstrings, and she ended up protesting the decision herself and managed to get the procedure approved.

I'll probably go to hell for that. Or for feeling almost disappointed when the mammogram was negative and I didn't have breast cancer. After all, if I had cancer, the "cosmetic" surgery I was scheduled for would have become instantaneously necessary surgery. My insurance company would no longer have considered it elective.

It was a momentary, stupid thing to think, that I was willing to trade cancer for eight thousand dollars' worth of surgery.

Then I felt terribly guilty. While I was selfishly trying to game the insurance system, a friend of mine was learning she needed a double mastectomy and breast reconstruction.

We went through very similar surgeries, but nothing about our experiences was the same.

Hopefully my ill-advised wish for breast cancer will never come true.

Even after the surgery I have some breast tissue left. They leave some of it behind, to provide the natural contours of a man's chest. So I'll always retain some risk of getting breast cancer, and I'll need to continue checking for lumps. And I'll almost always be the only guy getting a mammogram wherever I go for my screenings.

DIANE

I wasn't at all surprised that Jacob was hoping something was there on the mammogram that required the insurance company to cover surgery. We knew (know) dozens of trans people personally who have battled insurance companies and walked away the loser, never getting surgery that is very much medically necessary to many transgender people. Plenty of guys do fundraisers for years to come up with the money for chest surgery. If you can't self-raise it and you can't get insurance to cover it, the cost of surgery can be astronomical to an ordinary working class (or even middle-class) person. A lot of trans women we know who have had gender transition surgery (and for them it's not just top and bottom surgery but often facial feminization surgery, shaving down the Adam's apple, and more) could only afford to do so because of their higher (pre-transition) salaries. Of course plenty of trans women, especially women of color, are forced into sex work just to be able to afford hormones and breast implants.

So over the years we've heard plenty of acts of desperation because it's just unthinkable for many (but not all) trans people to live in a body they feel is incongruous with their self-image. When Jacob was having crazy thoughts, I too was exploring the craziness. What were the costs to fly to Thailand for the surgery (it's cheaper there), or what is the safety in driving down to the border and doing the procedure in Tijuana (a more common spot for inexpensive breast augmentation surgery, but surely removing them, I thought, couldn't be as complicated).

Jacob was worried about the money; he's generally always worried about the money because for many years we just never had any. Our "scrimp and scrape" twenties actually lasted until we were forty, I think—niche-publishing editor's salaries are rarely hefty—so money was always tight. And when you have two hundred grand in student loans and old medical bills, it feels crazy to spend another ten thousand on removing a body part.

Jacob would talk to me about being conflicted, his deep desire to have chest surgery versus his concern that it would cost us so much out-of-pocket. I felt for him but didn't share that concern. I knew that at this juncture, we had to do the right thing for Jacob, for his mental health and for his physical health. And we found a great surgeon (she's since retired) who did wonderful work, and I think it was the first time Jacob ever withstood any pain without great complaint. I knew he was hurting, but in a weird way, it was almost as if he felt like this was a pain that really earned him something. He's always been a sensitive sort when it comes to pain of any kind, but after the surgery, it almost felt like he was proud of this pain so he wasn't complaining, and whatever pain he was in he withstood with aplomb.

Having what is essentially a double mastectomy is no easy feat. For cancer patients, I'm sure it's far, far worse, in part because they are removing diseased tissue then following it up with chemotherapy and radiation and more. (And presumably they want to keep their breasts.) But even for guys like Jacob, it's painful, and after the surgery you're in bed for two weeks with a giant binder bandage around your chest, unable to lift your arms up, sometimes with drains attached to the incisions so fluid buildup literally drains out of your body. (So yeah, it's gross too, as are all surgeries just because they deal with icky things like blood and puss and medical stuff. Proof I could never be a doctor.) It hurt Jacob any time one of the dogs tried to jump on him in the bed (which happened far too often those two weeks because our Chihuahuas do not understand the word "no"), and it was painful when he tried to sit up or lift himself off the toilet. But he managed well. I did too.

I've been a caretaker, I think, since we came together. Jacob and I love tubing—jumping on a tractor inner tube and floating down the river. I remember our first year together, we went tubing down the Portneuf River through Lava Hot Springs, Idaho, with a few of our friends. We rode the small white-water portion of the river, then hit a slow but steady stream. We decided to float it longer than we had before and ended up hitting a patch where it slowed to a crawl. Then the skies turned dark and it began to thunder, so we knew lightning wouldn't be far behind. But because we weren't in a place where we could climb out of the riverbank and hike back to our car, our only option was to move forward. Fortunately the Portneuf isn't that deep, and where we were stranded, the water was about waist-high. So we jumped out of our inner tubes and began to hike down river, dragging the tubes behind us and hoping for a landing where we could climb out. But Suzy was chilled, shaking and unable to keep moving forward. So I picked her up and carried her myself, at least a mile, down the river. That set a standard where I would always be the strong one, the one who could be counted on to suck up and do what needed to be done.

And that's what I did when Jacob had his top surgery. I did what I needed to do. I had to look at his scars to check the incisions for infection, putting on the antibiotic creams after the stitches were removed. That wasn't easy for me because it was a post-surgery chest, stitched, sort of bloody and off-color, and shapeless. I was happy for him but also found myself tearing up frequently during that time. This person had been previously the owner of a pair of tits I greatly enjoyed looking at (and doing more than looking), and now, well, in their place was a chest I didn't recognize, one that wasn't quite "done" because it needed weeks to recover. I put on a positive face because he was so excited about getting one step closer to a body, and a life, that finally felt right.

Interesting note, after we had Jacob's surgery in Palo Alto, California, the state passed a law that requires medical insurance companies to cover transition-related medical care, including gender reassignment surgeries. Oregon, Colorado, and the District of Columbia have a similar law, and 25 percent of all Fortune 500 companies have the same requirement for their insurers. Clearly, the tide is changing, but it's certainly not fast enough for many trans people around the country. The last statistics I recall reading, from a San Francisco Department of Public Health study, said that more than 50 percent of transgender people did not have any form of health insurance.

Today I'm thrilled that Jacob is now covered by good insurance in a state that bars gender exclusions because now that he's a man, I worry about all the things that kill men several years earlier than women. I'm too set in my ways now to become a widow.

CHAPTER SIX

HOMICIDE

JACOB (SUZY)

I'm a murderer. I consciously, deliberately caused a person's life to end. But I'll never be punished for it. No prosecutor will ever charge me—not for premeditated murder or even negligent homicide—because no corpus delicti, no body of proof exists.

Her parents *could* file a wrongful death suit against me—they might even win—but I guess they like me too much, or maybe they just know I don't have enough money to make it worthwhile. I still see her parents every other year and they act happy to see me—I'm like a son to them—but they're still mourning the daughter they lost.

Wrongful-death suits exist because the law recognizes that our lives don't just belong to us; they also belong to our families. Our parents and spouses have expectations attached to our lives, plans for our futures, and when we die, those are snuffed out. Wrongful-death suits put a price on those lost expectations, on salaries never earned, on children never conceived.

At least most families still have memories of their loved ones that they can cherish. But her parents feel guilty about dwelling in the past. How do they mourn her and still keep me in their lives?

Her parents have mixed feelings about their memories, as though my actions have turned everything in her past into a lie.

I don't *feel* like a cold-blooded killer.

If anything, I feel like I helped her commit suicide. She made this decision as much as I did.

But my hand injected the poison that killed her. She embraced her death, even though it was painfully slow. She told her friends and family what was coming. She even blogged about the experience, about the signs of her death that slowly appeared.

Her parents knew what she wanted. They probably thought she was crazy, that she needed psychiatric treatment. They knew she was seeing a psychiatrist and that the shrink actually supported her decision, but that just led them to consider the doctor crazy too, to believe the whole system was crazy, a product of kooky California.

It took forever to kill her.

Hours passed. Days passed. She died slowly. Every two weeks I injected a little more of the poison. Weeks and then months passed, and she just wouldn't die.

But I was determined to end her life. And eventually, I won out. Suzy was just gone, leaving her parents haunted by one question: had she ever existed at all?

❖

That's how it feels to my parents. Maybe it sounds overblown, because I'm still here, and I'm the person they conceived, the one my mom gave birth to. And certainly their pain isn't comparable to someone whose child has passed away. But they still *feel* like their daughter died, like she's dead, because of me.

My chest-reconstruction surgery was the proverbial nail in Suzy's coffin. And while she stills exists in their memories, they find it difficult to speak about her in the past. What do they say? What pronoun do they use? How do they talk about their daughter when she no longer exists? How do they talk about their son's past when he sprang to life fully formed as a thirty-eight-year-old?

It's almost like something disrupted the time line. The line stretching from their daughter's birth to her post-forty-year-old future was abruptly severed. Another, parallel line sprang up. Starting at the moment I first decided to transition, this current time line has no past.

If there is a universe in which my parents, Wayne and Judy Minshall, gave birth to a son instead of a daughter, it isn't this one. Or is it? What do we make of a trans person's past? Have I always been the same person? Even once I came to know myself as a girl? Even when I bled and developed breasts? Even when I came out as a lesbian? Am I that same person today?

Was I always a boy, confused by his conflicting physicality and others' perception of him? Or was I a little girl who was raised a tomboy, developed an attraction for other women, and eventually convinced myself that I couldn't really be a girl if I felt so at odds with my body and the social roles society dictated for me?

The fact that our society is still screwed up when it comes to women doesn't help psychologists correctly identify when the female-bodied person in front of them is actually transgender instead of simply responding to societal pressures on women to look and behave a certain way. I remember a therapist telling me it was common for women to feel this way, that many women hated their bodies and didn't like being forced into the boxes that women were relegated to.

How could I call myself a feminist yet abandon the female sex? Why couldn't I just fight to change societal norms instead of surrendering, accepting the misogynistic view that women were one particular way? Why did I have to become a man instead of just being a different kind of woman?

These questions aren't easy to answer—at least for me. Some trans men and women know with utter certainty that they've always been male or female, and that their bodies were a lie, a birth defect that needed to be corrected. And other trans people feel like they were one sex and have transitioned into the other. Some trans people believe they've become an entirely different sort of being, neither male nor female, but something utterly new and modern, like a third sex. And still others—including many of those who identify as two-spirit—never undergo any kind of medical intervention because they believe society, not something within our biological makeup, makes us feel at odds with our bodies.

Can we all be right? Can we all be wrong? (If it seems I'm being a bit vague or un-pin-downable, I am. As a trans person I worry that, as one of the few visible trans people, I'll be taken as representing all trans folk. But we're a very large and diverse community.)

Mostly I feel like the same person I was when I was Suzy, like my life has been a quest of self-discovery and I've slowly worked through different identities like Goldilocks and the bowls of porridge, trying different ones in hopes of finding one that was "just right."

I say "mostly" because I believe hormone treatments have also made me a different person.

I *am* a different person on testosterone than I was when my system was flooded with estrogen.

As a feminist, this fact surprised me the most about transitioning: there is definitely a biological component behind the differences between women and men.

In women's studies classes I'd learned that nurture rather than nature causes the differences between the sexes and that by treating boys and girls differently, society creates differences between men and women. I'd certainly witnessed that socialization in practice, how the minute a baby is born in our culture we start differentiating between boys and girls. We dress boys in blue, girls in pink; we give boys cars and girls dolls.

Of course exceptions do exist. My parents let me wear shorts instead of dresses; they let me play with Matchbox cars instead of dolls and bought me an electronic football game instead of an Easy-Bake Oven.

I say "let me" because I believe I desired those things, and they gave them to me *because* I desired them.

But it could have been the complete opposite.

I could have wanted those things because they were given to me. My tomboyish mother or my sonless father could have valued masculine traits and interests and could have (consciously or not) rewarded me when I showed an appreciation for those things, thus reinforcing my interest in them. As the second-born child, I could have simply been differentiating myself from my older sister, gravitating to things she didn't like as a way of avoiding competition, creating my own niche in the family ecosystem.

I certainly don't doubt that socialization plays a role in determining who we are or why men value sports and women are better at sewing. I know that how children are treated and what parents and society expect of them impacts who they are enormously.

But I also know that once I started testosterone I also started changing. I don't just mean that I started getting hair in weird places or that fat redistributed itself on my frame—although both of those things did certainly occur. I mean that the psychological and mental side effects of testosterone dosing surprised me.

I used to be much more emotional. In fact, I used to have no emotional immunity. I would catch Diane's emotional states. Well, at least her negative ones. If she got upset and cried, soon I'd be upset and crying too. I cried *a lot*. In fact, I often felt at the mercy of my emotional ups and downs.

I don't anymore.

Diane says I've gotten duller. I liken it to being wrapped head to toe in neoprene. Testosterone literally makes your skin thicker. And it seems to do so metaphorically as well.

One of the first things my mother said, after I came out trans, was, "Men aren't known for their empathy."

It wasn't a warning. But maybe it should have been. My mom was saying that I'd always empathized with people who were different, which indicated that my brain was *not* male and therefore I was not trans.

It's true, I have been overly empathetic, getting upset at the way other people and animals are treated. Perhaps that was because I could empathize with those who were different because I was also different. Or maybe I didn't have good boundaries and couldn't tell where I ended and another person began. Or maybe I couldn't read other people's emotional cues, and instead I just projected my emotions onto them, which made it seem like I was empathizing.

When I was a child, my mother thought I might be autistic. She told me this when I came out as trans. Whatever the reason for my particularly heightened sensitivity to others' pain, to me it felt more like a handicap than a superpower.

Not empathy itself. Empathy is undervalued in our society. In fact many psychologists believe that a lack of empathy is at the root of many criminal behaviors—especially violent and sexual behaviors. Criminals, abusers, and Fortune 500 CEOs rarely put themselves in the shoes of their victims or share the pain of anyone else.

Then again, we live in a society of sharks like those unempathetic loan officers, politicians, billionaires, and other criminals. Maybe being empathetic is a disadvantage in this world. Maybe assuming other people share your emotional range and ability to care for others is just as pointless as wondering if your hamster is jealous of your new red hat.

Regardless—what I was afflicted with went way beyond empathy to a personalization of experiences and pains that weren't my own. Reading accounts by Holocaust survivors nearly killed me. Reading stories about mentally disabled children who'd been bullied, abused, or even killed helped give me an ulcer as a ten-year-old and sent me to my first therapist after my little sister was born with Down Syndrome.

Watching movies and TV shows has been particularly difficult. Having spent most of my childhood without access to a television meant I didn't develop any of the natural resistances and tolerances that most people build up over years and years of being exposed to it.

In college I couldn't finish watching movies where women were the victims of violence, like Jodie Foster's *The Accused* (in which a woman is gang-raped), and for different reasons, sometimes, even now, I have to leave the room when certain TV shows are on because I feel embarrassed for a character on the show.

❖

Growing up I often felt, and was frequently told, that I was just "too sensitive."

It got in the way of my ability to function in the world. It was like walking out the door without skin, with all of my sensitive nerve endings exposed to stimuli bombarding them from every direction. Like the cacophony of noises that knocks Bill Murray to his knees when he steps out onto a New York City street in *What About Bob*.

While I certainly wouldn't have denied being empathetic or even "too sensitive" when I first came out, at the time I questioned that it had anything whatsoever to do with my having a "female" or a "male" brain. In fact, with a background in women's studies I doubted there was enough of a difference between men and women's gray matter to even suggest the existence of a "male brain."

(I still don't believe our brains are necessarily all that different, and Rosalind Barnett and Caryl Rivers, the authors of *Same Difference: How Gender Myths Are Hurting Our Relationships, Our Children, and Our Jobs*, do a great job dispelling many of the statistical arguments made to support the existence of an unbridgeable distance between men and women.)

I've been tricked into most of my life lessons, transitioning being a prime example.

The one incarnation of a "male brain" that I accepted concerned gender assignment. Like many trans people, I believe that due to some chemical changes *in utero*, my body developed with female sexual characteristics while my brain developed with male characteristics, which is why I can't shake the cognitive certainty that I'm supposed to be male.

But, because my brain already thought it was male, and because feminist scholars had discounted the impact of biology on fundamental differences between the sexes, I didn't think hormone treatments would change much.

They did and they didn't. Testosterone didn't mold me into an entirely new person. It didn't make me talk like an action hero, or become addicted to working out, or discard my feminist heritage, or scratch my balls, burp loudly, swear like a trucker, and find fart jokes funny.

But it did change me, and one of the most dramatic ways was in dulling my senses.

Testosterone really does literally thicken your skin. It makes it rougher and less sensitive. Even my fingertips are less sensitive than they were before. It's like there is now a barrier between the world and me, as though I'm sheathed head to toe in a giant condom.

And my thicker skin carries over into the metaphoric. Just as my nerve endings are now protected behind a thicker layer of skin, so too are my emotional nerves. My emotional range has narrowed, the ups and downs have evened out, feelings flattened and quieted.

❖

I sometimes find myself truly, deeply not giving a rat's ass about the feelings or judgments of people who I would have—at the very least—had the decency to feel guilty about not caring for.

I'm not as good of a friend as I used to be. I don't keep up with my e-mail; I don't call people. The truth is before college I had very few friends. At Earlham College I made a number of really close friends, and at the time I was certain we'd be friends forever. That hasn't proved to be true.

Since then I haven't made a lot of close friends, and all together, I can count the people I think of as truly close friends on the fingers of one hand.

And I've always been a bit of a misanthrope.

Maybe I reacted to growing up a friendless outcast. Maybe my environmentalism or my deepening sense that humans are like a cancer on the planet, consuming all the natural resources, driving species into the black night of extinction and destroying the world, caused my attitude.

Don't get me wrong, I see the value in *people*—in specific, unique individuals; in cultural contributions, in our arts and music—but as a whole, as a species our cumulative impact has been to pretty much wreck the place. (And plenty of individuals do awful things to other people, sometimes thoughtlessly, sometimes deliberately with malevolent foresight, sometimes just spewing vile word daggers out into the Internet.)

It's not that we couldn't solve our problems and the problems we've unleashed on the world. We could. But something stops us. When it comes down to it, doing the tough thing, the right thing, just seems too difficult. Evolution also plays its part. We've evolved to be highly attuned to and skilled at responding to immediate threats. As a species, we're great in emergencies and disasters that unfold quickly, like hurricanes, fires, collapsing buildings, or being chased by a pride of lions.

But we're not that skilled at responding to future threats or to disasters that slowly unfold, like climate change or depleting our natural resources or, hell, even our future retirement needs. We'll respond quickly to changes that are going to happen in the next month or year, but ten years out seems like a lifetime away, even though it arrives much quicker than we imagine. Um—I'm not really sure how this ties into my point about empathy. I think this was just a huge digression. This is how my thought process works. It's kind of scary, I know. I just wanted to say that I think I'm less empathetic than I was before my hormone treatment. But I don't want to fabricate a past in which I'm depicted as a super-caring, benevolent person, either.

I've always felt a little like an outsider to the human race—a feeling that my parents' decision to get rid of TV when I was seven didn't help. That action made us miss the typical American socialization. My sister and I were outsiders. We didn't share cultural touchstones with our classmates because so many of the common experiences shaping them were being shared via television—be it popular sitcoms like *Laverne and Shirley* or miniseries like *Roots* (or exposure to diversity that occurred because of shows like *Roots*) or historic moments like the Columbia shuttle explosion or even exposure to products (Ginsu knives) and advertisement campaigns (Remember *Where's the beef?* I don't).

And my medical issues didn't help my sense of being other—including being allergic (as a child) to many things in nature and my gender dysphoria. All those elements influenced my sense that I wasn't like other people and therefore couldn't expect normal relationships with them. Not until my student exchange in Germany and later college did I finally find groups of people I clicked with. It hasn't happened a lot since, and every time it does I'm both pleasantly surprised and concerned it won't last.

Still, I think testosterone has made me even more remote and closed off to new friendships.

I just care less now.

DIANE

We were on a radio show talking about our books, being interviewed by some nice journalist who asked me about the difference between being married to a man and a woman. And I blurted out that Jacob was duller. Everyone laughed and nobody has let me live it down since, everyone seeing it as such a slam on him.

But I don't think it was. I think it's an honest assessment of a sort of flattening of his emotional state, a desensitization of his feelings and his physicality. He doesn't have highs and lows the way he used to. He's not prone to talking things out as much as he did a decade ago. Those hours of "lesbian processing" we did with all-night conversations about our hopes and dreams and feelings and hurts, yeah, those are all over. A person without emotional drama may be healthier, but they are also more boring. And so is Jacob. I love him and he still makes me laugh and lust and all the things he did before, but these days if anyone is shrill with excitement or wailing at the top of her lungs over a sad movie, it's me, not him. Things don't affect him the same way, but if they do, his reaction seems angry rather than anything else. He always says he's not angry, he can't describe how he is feeling, and maybe it's just that frustration, confusion, disinterest, and a host of emotions code as "anger" to me. Still his expression is stonier, less communicative, and it cuts me to the bone whenever he says, "It seems like I can't talk to you anymore," which I've heard a handful of times in recent years.

He can't feel things physically the same way either anymore. If I say, "Feel this," and point to an area on my arm or hand, for example, he touches it with a heaviness that tells me he can't quite feel the same way he could before. His literal touch is no longer light; he can no longer just graze my arm with his fingertips because that doesn't give him the same sensation any more—and his touch doesn't give me exactly the same sensation any more either, simply because it's rougher. I don't know how many times I've tried to show him a bump or a rash or something weird, and he can see it but can't feel it. Every part of him that was lean and, much to his chagrin, delicate, is now wider, thicker, stronger.

It reminds me of the complaints one of my girlfriends used to have about boys in high school, how their touch was so tough and clumsy, how ham-fisted they always were. I wonder now if it's really simply hormones that create that gender difference. Before he transitioned, Jacob could lightly touch my cheek with the back of his hand or push my hair off my neck for a kiss, and it was so tender, so sweet. He doesn't really do those things with any recurring frequency now (look, we've been married twenty-three years, so just finding time to make out is a struggle some days), but if he did those things still, I don't know if it would be as soft and tender or if it'd be more…well, simply, masculine.

It's an interesting change, his change, his emotional flattening, which took me years to get used to. Sometimes I still struggle with it. Sometimes I want to be able to look at his face and know that he's experiencing sheer joy or pure sadness, but I can't tell. There are no huge guffaws now, or crying jags, just a steady, even keel that makes him happy but can confound me. Scientists didn't know until a 2006 study proved it, but hormones required for gender change (the actual testosterone given to transgender men or the estrogen given to trans women) actually changes their brains. The study showed that stria terminalis of the hypothalamus of trans patients was the same as their gender identity after the hormones were administered. Since the area they studied in the stria terminalis is associated with a person's response to anxiety and stress response (as well as inhibition with strangers) I can see how some of Jacob's changes are purely hormonal; and since he is generally less anxious and less stressed, it's a very good thing.

But having a partner whose emotions aren't on the surface, who reads as guarded even though he's not, is tough. We've long heard jokes from male comics about women who want to talk, want to know their every thought, and sadly, I'm now one of those women. I don't think I ask any more questions than I used to ("What are you thinking?" being the classic), but the answers are different now that I have a husband instead of a wife. For example, "nothing" is always the reply to the above query, but two decades ago it might have more likely led to an esoteric conversation about our place in the world. But is that the difference of being with a man, being with someone twenty-three years, or now being in our mid-forties? Who knows?

JACOB (SUZY)

Before I transitioned, Diane and I both seemed susceptible to communicable emotions. If one of us was upset, afraid, sad, or what have you, we'd invariably "give" our feelings to each other. Also, say, I'd get mad at something—it didn't even have to be something Diane did or said; it could be something that happened at work or something that made me mad at myself—but the moment I expressed difficult emotions, Diane would become so upset I'd end up having to console her. Sometimes I'd stew about that afterward, about why I couldn't just experience my emotions without having to apologize for them. Even now Diane is especially sensitive to certain things like raised voices and harsh tones.

Things are different now. I just don't feel so sensitive, so emotional, and I'm not really susceptible to other people's emotions. I don't catch Diane's feelings. Overall, I find it such a relief to not be knocked around by emotional tides, but I recognize that I'm also less sympathetic to those who continue to be battered by the relentless waves. When I hear a kid whine about something I'm much more likely now to instantly feel like responding with a good old "Stop crying or I'll give you something to cry about" or "Grow up and stop being such a baby!" I don't say those things because I know they aren't appropriate to say to a kid (although we both heard them plenty as kids), but I think them, which is guilty new terrain for me.

I'm not as tolerant of emotional sensitivity these days. It annoys me. I feel like it's a sign of immaturity—even when I remind myself how I experienced those types of swings all the time, well into my thirties, and they had nothing to do with my immaturity. Nor did such mood changes reveal a lack of diligence. My ingrained misogyny is raising its head, equating emotions with immaturity. Can testosterone unlock subconscious misogyny?

Still, with my subdued emotions, we have fewer spats. And while I'm not as empathetic, in other ways I'm actually more understanding and am able to console Diane when her emotions overwhelm her because I'm not fighting my own.

It's like that episode of *Futurama* where the professor forces the robot Bender to feel Lela's emotions and then Bender is useless in a fight because he's curled up in fear and sadness. So many times when we were younger, Diane and I would get scared about some unknown noise at night and escalate ourselves into a panic. I couldn't just go check out the noise and reassure her because I was afraid too. The same emotional contagion would happen in our fights.

Now Diane's tears are no longer contagious. Instead, sometimes I catch myself wondering what she's getting so upset about. I don't think I'm an asshole. I just no longer can understand why she's upset. I'll think about what happened or what I said or what she just watched and compare it to her emotional state—like weighing the two on a pair of scales—and it just won't make sense to me. They won't seem equivalent. If I didn't know her so well, if I didn't remember that I used to get as upset as she does in these circumstances, I might even wonder if she could be faking, if she could be over-exaggerating for some reason.

Before I started hormone treatments a number of acquaintances warned me that testosterone would turn me into a raging, violent idiot. If that actually happened I certainly haven't been aware of it. Maybe I'm now too stupid to notice.

I don't *feel* like I've gotten angrier. But Diane might disagree.

When I do get upset now, she's more likely to interpret my emotional state as anger. It's like all my fear and sadness and disappointment and frustration now gets displayed as anger. Like my male face can show only two emotions at opposite ends of the spectrum: happiness and anger.

And now that I have a more narrow emotional range, it seems like maybe my range of emotional expressions has also narrowed.

I also know that Diane reacts differently to my emotional displays now that I'm a man. She often has a gut reaction to what she interprets as anger. Her gut reaction is fear. I see it reflected in her face. It passes quickly, but it always makes me feel awful. It's like a punch to my stomach. I hate that women sometimes cross the street to avoid me now. But I despise making the woman I love feel afraid.

I'm trying to keep my negative emotions in check, not venting or lashing out in a way that I might have when I was younger. We don't do slammed doors or raised voices at our house. Raised voices have always made Diane nervous. They're like thunder for her; they signal a coming storm. And while, in nature, the sound of thunder travels slower than the light of a strike, for Diane, thunderous voices predict a different kind of strike. They predict imminent violence.

Ironically, while my emotional outbursts can scare Diane, I experience fear far less often than I did prior to transitioning. I remember often feeling afraid, especially when Diane and I were younger. I was afraid of strangers, of men, of the creaks and bumps and sounds in the night. I couldn't sleep sometimes because of fear.

I do know that some of that fear faded as we got older and I became more self-confident. I gained confidence over the years, especially when I became a park ranger and went through a police-academy-style training program. I understand so much better now how men who doubt their own masculinity are drawn to these jobs. I can understand why people who want to prove their masculinity often end up serving time in the military or on the police force. Not only does the image itself provide an effective cover of your secret fears about your masculinity, but those kinds of situations really do "make you a man" in these particular ways. You're forced to deal with intense, sometimes terrifying situations. They provide training and opportunities for skill development and force you to accept responsibility. I got this training while I was still identified as a woman.

I'm not sure exactly how to explain it, but when I was a ranger, a lot of times I was scared and just wanted to turn and walk away, but I'd remind myself there was no one else. It was my job to put out that fire, rescue a stranded hiker, go into that darkened restroom, help the car-crash victim despite my low tolerance for the sight of blood. No one else was going to step in and do those things for me. The buck stopped with me, so to speak.

So I developed confidence in my abilities and some of my insecurities about life faded away, but once testosterone kicked in, they evaporated. And I got to see something else. It wasn't that men were braver, feeling the same fear but still carrying on courageously. No, apparently they're often spared the terror itself. I'm not saying men are never afraid, because they are, and I'm also aware that I'm generalizing an awful lot. But on testosterone I'm simply more secure, more confident.

Social norms may also influence some of this difference. After all, two women simply *are* at greater risk of being victimized than a man and a woman are. Whether it's a patriarchal agreement between men not to fuck with another man's female property or just an assumption that a man will offer more resistance to an attack, perpetrators are less likely to target a male-female dyad than two women.

Regardless of why it has faded, having less fear is wonderfully freeing. And it makes me a lot more convincing when I assure Diane, "It's okay, not to worry. It's just the wind, and I'll go out and check just to be sure."

❖

Don't get me wrong. This change doesn't mean that I'm fearless. I still worry about the state of the world. I still don't ride roller coasters. I still don't like heights. I still worry something will happen to our dogs. I still have moments when I'm terrified Diane will leave me, willfully or through an unexpectedly early death.

I'm still nervous in crowds of men, especially straight men. I'm still slightly afraid that someone will learn of my trans identity and react poorly. I'm still afraid that—because men now see me as another guy—I'll be caught in some situation that escalates to violence, say because I looked at some dude's girlfriend or somehow failed to show the proper respect. Although I now look like a native, I'm still learning male culture and men's language. I'm not entirely fluent or assimilated, and I still make cross-cultural missteps. Diane is great at helping me understand cultural norms, but sometimes I'm not even aware of the cultural expectation I've violated.

It's like adjusting to the "real" world after growing up without TV, or the year I spent in Germany when I arrived without knowing the language.

I'm still suspicious by nature. I am. I often question people's motives, especially those of strangers, and most especially those of male strangers who are nice to me. I immediately wonder what they want.

I've had to adjust to the way men speak to me now. Prior to transitioning, I thought the usual male-to-male greeting was a grunt and a head bob. But now men actually *talk* to me. I don't mean they tell me their deepest feelings or hold hour-long conversations. But they don't just pass me by. And they do more than just grunt "Hey."

I'm not quite used to it. It still strikes me as strange.

So, I *am* a different person than I was before my transition. But when I think of the past I see myself as a tomboy named Suzy, a butch-identified lesbian, a park ranger named Susannah. I think of myself as a formerly female-bodied person who suffered from gender dysphoria, whose physical sex didn't match their brain sex. I'm a guy named Jacob who was a once a girl named Suzy, a man who was never a little boy, a dude who went through puberty much later than my peers.

So what happened to Suzy? Is she dead? Did she ever really exist—did the daughter my mother imagined I would be ever exist? Even if I hadn't transitioned, would I ever have met her expectations? Or did my transition just force my parents to accept what had been true all along?

And have they *really* accepted it?

Maybe Suzy isn't dead at all. Maybe she's still alive on a farm in Idaho, in the house her father built, the barn-shaped house where they still talk about her, where my own parents still often refer to me by *her* name and *her* gender. Maybe that's why they can't stop calling me her name, especially when I'm not physically in front of them.

Maybe they fear that the minute they stop uttering her name she really will be gone. It will all become too real, and they'll have to really, truly accept that she's never, ever coming back.

Suzy is dead. Long live Suzy.

DIANE

The first few months of Jacob's transition were so much about him that I hardly had time to deal with my own emotions. I felt like I couldn't show any disappointment, denial, or concern either to him, our family, or the outside world. Ever since we got together, I've always felt pressure to represent well—I've said the phrase, "I'm a model gay" even—and though I've always written about our relationship honestly, I've never spoken poorly of him, our relationship, or of any difficulties we had between us.

Once, when we first moved to San Francisco, we were homeless for six months, living out of our Volkswagen bus at a state park on the beach in Half Moon Bay. We'd drive that same bus to my office in the morning, a trek over the Santa Cruz Mountains, which always made me vomit. Jacob and our Border collie Free would hang out in the VW during the day, and then at night we'd all make the hour-long trek over the mountain back to the campground. We had very little money so we ate beans, cooked over a campfire every night, and skipped the other meals. Even then I didn't tell my family; I didn't see any reason to worry them over something they couldn't afford to help us with. We've gone through many tough times that we haven't shared with my family; Jacob talks to his mother more often about the downsides, but I'm always telling him to stop that. He has a different dynamic, though it's one I don't understand.

After Jacob's transition, not every family member or friend was accepting or happy about it so I had to become his champion and his cheerleader, a buffer to the world of hostilities against trans people, cheering every little kindness and absorbing (but not sharing with him) any indignity cast his direction.

It was a lonely time. Then when I could start to think about myself the change really hit me. It wasn't about his genitals, or his new male presentation, or even suddenly being perceived as straight (which is, or at least was, isolating for me as well). It was about the loss of shared women's space and the ability to share every single moment with another woman. It first hit me when we both went back to the gym. We usually went to the gym together a few times a week to swim, and we'd share a locker and all our stuff in one bag. We had our routine down to who locked the locker and who grabbed the towels. Suddenly I was alone in the locker room because he had to be with the boys and that nice co-dependent cocoon-like bond we had was gone and for the rest of my life I would be doing things like this by myself. It seems silly to say out loud, but I just broke down sobbing that first day in the locker room because I was completely overwhelmed and unprepared for that change. I had been with a woman my entire adult life, and I liked the way that two women together can share the world together. And now I knew I'd had lost that.

Over the years I've gotten used to this, the first year clearly being the worst. His transition has changed places we go and things we do. We used to go to spas together a lot, but since so many of them are sex-segregated (because the hot pools, showers, and such are clothing-optional), it's no longer fun for either of us. Now if I go to a spa, I take a female friend. Since Jacob is no longer welcome (nor should he be) in most women's spaces, I do the same if I go to those types of events. In San Francisco, which just may be home to the highest percentage of trans men and genderqueer individuals, a lot of events that were once women-only have opened up to trans men, so when it feels right Jacob will go with me. But he's a long-time supporter of women's space (he's one of those feminists who spelled women with a Y at one point), so he generally doesn't think men should be allowed in it (although we both argue vehemently that trans women certainly should). If you don't identify as a woman, you don't deserve to be in women's space—that's his logic. But, again, that's where I get penalized, because those are all events I would previously have shared with him, not over about-to-fall-asleep pillow talk after I come home, but literally with him at the event together.

We both lost something. He lost access to women's space, to the right to identify with the women he had identified with since childhood.

And I lost women's space too. I entered a world that was sex segregated to an absurd degree; I just didn't even realize that was the case until Jacob transitioned.

I lost a wife. But I did gain a husband. We found some benefits that were immediate and startling, and they both highlighted and underscored "heterosexual" privilege for me in a way a dozen textbooks never could. For one, as soon as we were perceived as a man and a woman instead of a butch woman and a femme woman, the level of street harassment we received dropped dramatically. In fact, I can't remember the last time it happened—not for several years at least. And all those hoops I went through every time I needed to visit him in the hospital or talk to a bill collector on one of his accounts? Yeah, those are gone forever. A small, singular one-word change opened up the world for me, and it made me sad to realize how many rights I had been denied that I'd just assumed weren't given to anyone without a hassle. That one-word change? From "wife" to "husband."

Chapter Seven

Making It Legal

JACOB (SUZY)

In March 2006, before the California Supreme Court's (pre-Prop 8) ruling declaring the ban on same-sex marriages unconstitutional, Diane and I got married for a fourth time. Diane says it was the fifth because we had a little private, semi-naked, moonlit ceremony our first year together. Either way, we've spent decades fighting for marriage equality, and this wedding changed everything. It was also for keeps. This was the first wedding the government couldn't take away from us, because I was an entirely different person.

In the thirteen months since our San Francisco City Hall wedding, I'd come out as transgender. I'd had surgery and had been on testosterone for months and had officially and legally transitioned from female to male. I'd legally changed my name and sex and proudly sported a California driver's license proving my new identity.

Legally becoming a man made the difference. Suddenly I could legally wed Diane. Not only would the state of California now recognize a union it had rejected less than a year prior, but the United States federal government would follow suit and recognize it as well. Now that we were no longer a same-sex couple we could take full advantage of the rights and responsibilities of legal marriage.

At first, we weren't sure if we should go through with it. Just because we suddenly *could* get married, did that mean we should? After all, many of our friends and comrades in arms still couldn't get married. The hundreds of couples who'd snaked through San Francisco City Hall the year previous (only to have their marriages annulled) were still being denied the right to wed. Most of them didn't have this new transgender loophole in their favor. Their love was no less real, their commitment no less valid, so how could we get married when they couldn't?

On the other hand, we've always jumped at the chance to validate our relationship. It would be out of character for us to pass up the opportunity now, when legal marriage was finally in reach.

DIANE

We had a lot of pondering to do though. We'd just spent sixteen years fighting for the right for same-sex couples to be able to marry, and now we had that privilege, but only because we were no longer a same-sex couple.

Would it be fair to our gay, bisexual, and lesbian friends if we got married when they still couldn't? We desperately wanted the extra thirteen hundred plus federal rights that married couples get, to know that I'd never again be barred from seeing Jacob in the hospital or making decisions about our joint credit accounts, to be sure that when I die I'll leave him everything I have and he won't have to pay taxes on it the way same-sex spouses still did. But I didn't want to be a traitor to the cause. By then straight celebrities like Angelina Jolie and Brad Pitt and Dax Shepard and Kristen Bell had decided not to marry until everyone could; should we do the same? (Kristen and Dax married in 2013, after the Supreme Court struck down the Defense of Marriage act and same-sex couples could marry in many areas.)

We talked with all our friends and colleagues and found, much to my relief, that they all thought we should do it, both to remind the world we'd already been married for sixteen years and to protect ourselves in places like our home state of Idaho, where Jacob's status as a man might always be on shaky ground without federal guidelines on trans rights.

So we decided to go for it, and I was tasked with planning the ceremony of my dreams, even though I'd never been one of those girls with big wedding dreams. As a kid I didn't even expect to get married. In high school I had all but decided to be "footloose and fancy free," an unrepentant slut without the baggage of kids or marriage shackles. If anything, I was mistress material. All of this is ironic, though, considering that I've mostly been in a series of long-term relationships since I was fourteen.

Planning the wedding was absolutely engaging, however, and I found myself going a bit bonkers with all the material I had. As I often do in life, I was planning our wedding while simultaneously using all my research information to put together a wedding issue for *Curve* magazine. Many, many of my best experiences have been an integral part of my writing. Every time I've gone to the Caribbean or South America or Disneyland, learned to snorkel, gotten a bikini wax (once was enough), or experienced some exotic body treatment like Watsu (think water shiatsu), I've done so as much for the article as for the experience.

Almost every travel experience I had after I turned twenty-two was the basis of an article at some point. My favorite of course was when the El Dorado Casino in Reno gave me a high-roller package, picking me up in their private jet for a twenty-minute flight from San Francisco to Reno, then putting me up in the largest suite in the hotel. The whole weekend was a scene from *Lifestyles of the Rich and Famous* and a glorious experience that became a fantastic article people still ask me about. I could see no reason for experiences to go undocumented, and writing about things allow Jacob and me to experience much more posh settings than my salary would ever allow.

The same is true for my wedding, which actually inspired several articles in more than one magazine. I'm lucky to have a spouse who admires and appreciates the importance of the media, because if he didn't it'd be a much lonelier world for both of us.

The most crazy-making part of wedding planning is that generally people can't seem to avoid going a bit overboard, no matter how level-headed they are. I had no preconceived notions, no childhood dreams, but as soon as I got all the books and magazines and online photo spreads and advice from people who give it unsolicited (which is everyone), I found myself so knee-deep in planning and budgeting and discovering ways to do what they said would cost forty thousand dollars on my two-thousand dollar budget, that for a brief moment I wondered if I should leave publishing and become a full-time LGBTQ wedding planner. Once the wedding and the wedding issue were done and printed respectively, that idea disappeared for good. It's now a box of research material and a few mementos that sits in our closet along with a gorgeous dress.

❖

The wedding was lovely.

I couldn't afford one of those expensive Vera Wang gowns, so I turned to eBay and found a dressmaker in Hong Kong who would make me a knockoff of a Monique Lhuillier gown that, at the time, was selling for almost six thousand dollars. The gown was fairly medieval-looking, with a corset top and wide princess bottom and long lace sleeves with lace bells at the end.

I was the only woman I knew getting married in California in the 2000s who actually had long sleeves on; funny, since most of the time I eschew sleeves altogether. The cost? A hundred and fifty dollars. Sure, the fabric was cheaper, but from the audience nobody could tell. It looked gorgeous, and I loved it all the more because of the price tag. I just hoped the labor had been the woman's own, not some poor exploited sweatshop worker's.

We studied Jacob's dad and mom's wedding photos, a rather subdued wedding, perfectly reminiscent of his pragmatic scientist parents, and noticed his dad was wearing a white tux, as were the groomsmen. It reminded me of a photo of my dad, maybe his senior-class photo. I'm not sure. But he's wearing a white tux and a bow tie, and he looks handsome but unformed, not yet the powerful, assured man I knew growing up. Jacob and I turned to each and knew instantly that he and his groomsmen would wear white tuxes; we agreed on pink ties and cummerbunds, a silent wink and nod to the world that Jacob was so confident with his masculinity now he could do something he never could do as a woman: wear pink.

I chose a bridesmaid dress I loved, a sleeveless candy confection that looks like it was perfect for the sixties, and offered my bridesmaids their choice of colors based on our 1980s retro wedding colors: pastel pink and lime green. It was as if we'd hired George Michael (or his 1980s band, Wham!) to be our wedding planner. But something about reclaiming all these memories from my teen years made the wedding fun and quirky and comforting for me. I loved the bridesmaid-dress design so much I even had one made for myself to wear at the reception. I rationalized that the dresses were so cute, the bridesmaids could wear them again and again. To this day, I think I'm the only person who's ever reworn her dress, but I have, several times, to garden parties and once, on laundry day, even to work.

We made cute but formal invitations, talked my colleague Sara Jane Keskula into being the wedding organizer the day of the wedding, and chose our wedding party carefully. The groomsmen were Jeff, my childhood boyfriend who to this day remains my BFF, even when we go months or years without talking; my brother Keith, who I wasn't raised with because he's twenty years younger than I am, but who I have so much in common with; my "nephew" Justin, who's actually the son of Florence, the woman people often mistake for my sister, but who's really my cousin and is the daughter my Aunt Luanne gave up for adoption in the 1960s.

Our last groomsman was Kelly, the friend Jacob had met at Midpen, with whom we'd managed to become good friends. She wasn't a lesbian when we met, but she certainly was one within a few months of meeting us. (I think we got a toaster oven for recruiting her into the lesbian nation.)

Our bridesmaids were tough to limit to five since we have so many wonderful women in our lives. But we narrowed it down to my BFF Athena (for both Athena and Jeff, this was our second wedding they were serving in as best man and maid of honor), as well as my sister Tanya (who I also didn't grow up with but have always tried to be part of her life since she was born), Elisa, another friend of Jacob's who was also a park ranger, my friend and one-time right-hand lady at *Curve,* Julia Bloch (now an academic and poet), and Jacob's little sister Jennye.

One of my photographers flew in from Portland to photograph us because I felt more comfortable in front of the camera lens with Kina Williams than almost anyone else, and my friend and one-time colleague Kathleen Hildenbrand, who owns her own super-hot salon, Lucky 13 in Columbus, Ohio, flew in to do my hair. Athena spent the day pampering me and making sure everything was okay. We went out of our way to find a Catholic wedding officiate who would also marry same-sex couples; we wanted a Catholic priest as a nod to Jacob's very Catholic parents, but we didn't want to reap a reward that wouldn't be offered to our friends for their weddings. Thankfully the White Robed Monks, a slightly more liberal order in California, believe in the sanctity of marriage equality.

We sent invitations—the first time we'd ever invited anyone in our families to a special event, in part because I didn't ever want to deal with the sting of rejection. For many years some of our family members were staunchly against our relationship, and I felt like if they rejected me on an occasion like this it would further disenfranchise us from them.

To our surprise, Jacob's parents and sisters all RSVPed, so we asked his mom and older sister to read during the ceremony and his little sister to be a bridesmaid. My stepmother Marlene and Tanya and Keith came up along with Keith's high-school girlfriend and

Tanya's two kids. Because they were always on a tight budget, I was astonished and honored that they spent the money to drive up and take off the weekend shifts they usually worked to be there.

As I was planning the wedding I was very cognizant of the discussions my stepmother Marlene had had with me when I was little about the importance of a wedding. She'd never had one; my father was her first marriage, and because he was smarting after his two divorces, he refused to actually "marry" Marlene, even though by common law they were married seven years into their now-thirty-five-year relationship. I remember Marlene humming that song "Chapel of Love" and talking to me about weddings with a little glisten in her eyes, so I kept that in mind, trying to make sure a lot of what we planned for the day would be stuff she'd be proud of, while staying true to our roots, and I put that song on the reception playlist.

My nephew James, then only three or four, was the ring bearer and so adorably had to be guided down the steps to where we were; my niece Adrianna, a year younger and equally cute, was the flower girl, tossing out reusable silk flowers. My brother walked me down the aisle and did a great job of making me feel comfortable (we cracked jokes on our way down) and making sure I didn't miss my father so much.

My dad didn't come. It's not that he didn't support our relationship. He was the first person to call Jacob my "co-pilot," a word I still use today because it's so apt, and he was one of the more accepting family members when we announced that Jacob was transitioning. (It may shock some, but the men on my side of the family were among the most accepting, possibly because it made sense to them that he'd want to be a dude.) But my father has a social-anxiety disorder. It's hard for him to be in the same room with a group of people, even if the people are his family members. Hanging out with strangers would be even worse.

He's had it since I was a kid, but I can see it's worsened greatly as he's grown older. So between traveling and being in a big group, my dad passed on this event.

But right before the wedding ceremony, as I was sitting there in this beautiful Greek glass-and-stone amphitheater on Central Lake in Foster City's Leo J. Ryan Memorial Park, getting a foot massage from Jacob and marveling at the gorgeous location we'd scored for two hundred and fifty dollars, Marlene handed me a cell phone, and my dad was on it.

He congratulated me and wished me luck and apologized for not being there. I teared up as we spoke, and my dad said something he often says, his awkward third-person acknowledgement of the love and distance that has always both divided and united us: "Daddy loves you."

My Aunt Luanne came on her own accord. If she hadn't, Jacob and I would have driven to Idaho and kidnapped her to make sure she was there on our special day. It was hard enough not having my grandmother alive to see me walk down the aisle. Not having Luanne there as well would have been excruciating. My aunt had been a demanding and exacting parental figure ("not too shabby" was her highest praise to me as a kid), pushing me to excel in a way no one else did. Thankfully, she's always been supportive of my relationships, and Jacob is as close to her as his own family. Maybe more.

My mother didn't come. Her support of us had always been up and down; some days her fundamentalist Christian beliefs and deeply internalized homophobia stopped her from being supportive or even acknowledging that Jacob was a man. I believe her absence at our wedding had more to do with her being unaware of how important and symbolic this wedding really was for us, but with her extensive mental-health issues it's always a crapshoot trying to understand how she feels about a certain issue. If I asked her today, my mom might say she didn't even know we got married.

Several of my colleagues or former colleagues turned friends were there and brought with them their individualism that I love. One polyamorous friend of mine, whom I now haven't seen in years, brought two dates: her husband and her boyfriend, both of whom lived with her in the same house. I admire anyone daring enough to go beyond the two-person rule and anyone (like her husband) who can welcome a triangular relationship and make it work for them. The three of them are now raising twins together.

We'd written our own vows. Jacob reminds me often that his said he'd "try" to be a good husband, thinking I'd made an error in my word choice there, a poor move on an editor's part. Mine outright promised everything except fidelity and obeying—the former a promise I hoped to keep but didn't want to break if I changed my mind, and the latter, a relic of earlier times that shouldn't be in anyone's wedding these days. I consider everyone but I obey no one. There was some crying, a native-American prayer, some Catholic scripture, silver rings with the Hebrew inscription from the *Song of Solomon* that read "I am my beloved's and my beloved is mine," and one moment in which we tried to release native butterflies but instead had to wake them up onstage and then watch two of them fly straight down my cleavage as I flailed about. It was videotaped, so my nieces and nephews will get a good laugh watching it when they're older.

As with any wedding, things went wrong at ours. My carefully orchestrated alternating pink and green color scheme petered out when we discovered the plates were missing. Sara Jane went and bought others but couldn't find anything to match my awesomely insane color scheme.

When we opened up the fancy porcelain wedding figures that go on top of the cake (which by the way was gorgeous and five layers high), they turned out to be a miniature blond woman and a black man, but we figured we'd just look all that more progressive.

Nobody else concluded that, so they asked us about it all day long. (Short answer: they were free.)

Two coworkers there were gossiping about my boss, who just happened to roll by and hear it all, and that certainly put a damper on things.

We bought all these vintage-themed fruit sodas instead of alcohol to both be hip and healthy and to make sure nobody overdid it. At least one of our friends was in recovery, and since booze isn't that important to us, we assumed everyone would be fine. But someone forgot the ice so the drinks were hot, and as soon as we hit the reception Jacob's dad was complaining so loudly about not having beer that my coworkers considered driving to a 7-11 just to shut him up. Of course the Idahoans couldn't believe we didn't stock beer at the reception.

And we heard that my aunt (the unofficial mother of the bride) and Jacob's mom had a minor scuffle over, I think, the proper way to cut the cake. That seemed the most normal of all the arguments.

All of that aside, it was a magical day.

JACOB (SUZY)

For years LGBTQ folks have been saying that civil unions and domestic partnerships aren't equivalent to heterosexual marriage. Having had both, I can honestly say that is true.

It didn't seem to matter that we'd been together sixteen years and participated in multiple ceremonies, including a pre-Prop 8 wedding at San Francisco's City Hall. Things changed with our Foster City wedding. Our families came. And they began to treat us differently.

But most of the differences came in the way strangers treated Diane and me both pre- and post-marriage. Store clerks *ooohed* and *ahhhed* about our upcoming nuptials. All it took was my male name and the simple word "husband" to persuade representatives of everything from credit-card companies to HMOs to reveal personal information about my wife, which had previously been denied me as her registered domestic partner of fifteen years. In small, barely perceptible instances throughout the day, our relationship was honored and respected once we were "really" married.

However, a June 2007 article in the publication *Catholic Daily News* suggested that I'd transitioned just to get married, to get around the rules against same-sex marriage. The funny thing is that other people have asked me this too: will lesbians transition so they can gain access to legal marriages?

I can't really imagine lesbians rushing en mass to become men, even if it would give them the legal privileges of marriage. Most lesbians I know actually like being women, physically. It's one of those things that do separate trans guys from lesbians, especially butch-identified lesbians.

Plus, few people would be willing to go through the convoluted steps required to medically transition, even if the change promises the potential of legal recognition. (And not all states recognize trans people as members of their preferred genders; some heterosexual trans folk are legally considered to be in same-sex relationships— this is one reason same-sex marriage is a trans issue.)

Consider if you'd be willing to commit to the following if it would grant you additional rights or protection: undergoing intensive talk therapy, legally changing your name, injecting yourself with hormones every two weeks—and dealing with the physical and emotional alterations the hormones bring, paying for expensive surgeries, and having your body—including your private parts—permanently surgically altered. Not to mention the weeks and months of recovery and, for some trans folks, the many additional surgeries needed to get everything functioning correctly and gender confirming.

Sure, maybe a few people might try to transition for the wrong reasons. That's why psychotherapy and medical evaluation are critical elements in the process. The professionals involved screen applicants to rule out other issues—psychological, physical, or otherwise. But trust me when I say this: lesbians are never going to claim gender dysphoria in order to marry. I sincerely hope that now that the Supreme Court has struck down the Defense of Marriage Act and seventeen states and counting have legalized same-sex marriage, I will stop hearing that question.

CHAPTER EIGHT

ANDROPHOBIA

JACOB (SUZY)

As I transitioned, I wasn't prepared for the level of androphobia (abnormal and persistent fear of men) among straight women. I understand that, at night, I might appear to be just another potential predator, but I'm surprised when it happens over the phone. Men are suspect even there.

I'm talking to an advice nurse. To a certain degree, my "hetero" marriage has opened up access to Diane's medical professionals. If it relates to an illness of some kind, like the flu, the word "husband" seems to grease the wheels and unlock doors.

If, on the other hand, I'm calling to discuss an injury, say my wife's broken toe, suddenly that same word causes everything to instantly shut down, like prison lockdown after an escape attempt. Rather than friendly and helpful service providers, suddenly I'm speaking to a very cold, suspicious, and tight-lipped regulator who demands to know *why* my wife can't come to the phone herself.

I say she's in an important business meeting and won't be available at all today and maybe not tomorrow either. I don't go into a long explanation about Diane asking me to call; nor do I detail the inner workings of magazine publishing or the meaning of the word deadline, or how missing said deadline with a printer can translate to costing tens of thousands of dollars. This nurse doesn't know me, doesn't know Diane. The bottom line is that often Diane won't call the advice nurse or the doctor's office; she'll keep limping or bleeding or whatever the problem is and work twelve-hour days until the magazine is done.

The advice nurse doesn't ask for an explanation, but she's clearly doubtful.

"She needs to come in," she announces.

"Okay, what if she can't get to the doctor? What should she do in the meantime?"

"She needs to come in," she repeats.

"Of course, but in the meantime? We wrapped her foot—"

"We don't like the toes taped to each other."

"Okay." I'm thrilled just to get a new answer. "The broken toe isn't actually taped to the other toes. We wrapped her whole foot."

Silence.

"Well, what would you tell someone who couldn't get to the hospital?"

"I'd tell them they needed to come in."

"What if they were trapped in a remote forest and couldn't get out?" I persist, imagining circumstances where a doctor wasn't immediately available.

"Then I'd tell them to keep their leg up and put ice on it, and get to a doctor."

Clearly this woman has never experienced the woods, remote or otherwise. I've never come across an ice machine in the middle of a forest. And she seems unfamiliar with the possibility that medical assistance might not be close by.

What if we were still living in ranger housing in the Santa Cruz Mountains? There's not a doctor, hospital, or medical clinic within a thirty-minute radius. That's why rangers like me were trained in emergency medical response.

During winter storms it wasn't uncommon for trees to come down and block driveways and even the main road. Decades ago the residents of Silicone Valley decided they didn't want to deal with high-capacity power lines defacing their view, so they pushed all the big power lines into the nearby mountains. Every year storms also knock down some of these highly dangerous lines, which have been known to spark fires and trap people in their homes.

I want to ask, "What if we were unable to get off the hill? What if we were trapped in our house? What if we were in New Orleans after Katrina? What if I'm with the government and I'm torturing a terrorist suspect and I can't exactly let the prisoner go for medical help, but being a good person I don't want his toe to fall off either, so I just want to know what to do while we wait for him to give up his terrorist buddies? What would you advise me then?"

(By the way, it took Diane six months to actually go see a doctor about that toe; when she did, she learned she had shattered her metatarsal joint and needed joint-replacement surgery. The doctor asked why it took her so long to come in and she said, "I was on deadline.") Back to the larger point though: now that I'm a man, apparently I'm suddenly more likely to break my wife's bones and be holding her hostage, preventing her from speaking on her own behalf. I get it. Men are the majority of perpetrators in our country; they're usually the one behind intimate partner violence. I'm now a suspect.

Something happens a year later when Diane breaks a glass and cuts her arm. At the hospital the nurses interrogate her: "Did someone do this to you? Do you want to tell us something? Did you cut yourself on purpose? Were you trying to commit suicide? Is someone at home hurting you? Did your husband do this?"

For all her protestations, I can't help but wonder if her medical file contains a note suggesting Diane may be the victim of domestic violence.

The other place people watch me suspiciously is around children. I can no longer wave or make funny faces at the kids in line at the grocery stores without engendering evil-eye stares from their mothers, who pull their kids closer to them or actually shift their bodies in between me and their kids, like a barricade to keep my dangerous gaze from meeting their innocent ones. It's one of those things that you don't realize is a privilege when you're female-bodied, and you don't realize you'll miss it when it's gone. Being feared, instead of fearful, isn't an easy transition.

DIANE

Certain things were a struggle, especially during the first year Jacob was taking testosterone, when he embodied that hazy ground between man and woman. Or maybe it was between boy and man.

We were waiting for those first facial hairs to grow in, for his skin to thicken, for his muscles to develop. The struggle was especially intense in San Francisco, and even more so when we'd attend lesbian events and everyone would assume Jacob was simply a butch woman.

He didn't seem to mind being mistaken for a lesbian. But somehow I did. I was constantly worried this misconception would undermine his newfound feelings of maleness. Being a relatively tall woman, Jacob actually began to pass as male quite quickly. But, sometimes, being identified as a man made things even worse. It was difficult for people to understand why a man was at a lesbian event.

When it was clear he was there with me and we were a couple, they couldn't understand why a presumably straight couple was at a queer bar or representing a lesbian magazine. Once on a press trip, as we were trying out several new restaurants to critique for a travel article, we had a memorable experience.

The manager of one place asked about *Curve*, and I explained that it was a lesbian publication. Her brow knitted and she looked back at Jacob.

"This is my husband," I said.

Her puzzlement only increased. "But this is a magazine for lesbians?"

"Yes."

"But you two are—?"

"Married," I supplied.

She shook her head.

"He hasn't always been a guy," I finally said, falling back on my over-sharing. "When we got together he was still a girl."

She seemed even more baffled but just gave up trying to understand why I edited a lesbian magazine if I was married to a man, even one who'd been a woman for most of our relationship.

Sometimes these queries contained an air of patronization and homophobia as well.

One of my best lesbian friends even said to me, "Maybe now you can go work at a real magazine." As though my apparently now-dwindling lesbianism was the only reason I'd worked twenty years in LGBTQ media, and without it I'd be free to envelop myself in the world of mainstream women's magazines. I reminded her that I'd left mainstream publishing to work in LGBTQ media. But the underlying offense and its internalized homophobia still clung to me and still stings today. It also reminds me of how often gays and lesbians forget the "B" in LGBTQ. Nearly all the time people treated me like a former lesbian who was now straight, instead of assuming I was a bisexual woman and still validly a part of the LGBTQ world.

Jacob and I struggled with words—not pronouns, but literally the word "husband." It felt wrong and foreign to both of us. For sixteen years I'd called Suzy my "wife," so transitioning to "husband" should have been a natural evolution. But Jacob and I both disliked the attendant baggage and the built-in patriarchal feel of the word. I'd loved being a wife to another woman. I'd never planned to be a wife to some man. *Never.*

Jacob felt the awkwardness too. At one point, uncomfortable with being a husband in a world of wives, he asked me to call him my partner. Since I'd long ago discarded the word "partner" because I found it too clinical, too businesslike for romantic love and companionship, I was reluctant to do so. But I tried, and in less than a week, I erupted with an "I can't do it anymore" tantrum so tearful and heartfelt that Jacob, I think, felt bad for even suggesting it.

More disconcerting than losing my wife was the idea that my relationship would become so sterile I could describe it with the word partner. It was a hard one to explain to many folks, though, as I have many friends and colleagues who use the word happily; they like the egalitarianism and feminism built into the word, a phrase that comes to marriage without the baggage of ownership that "wife" has. I get that. I just always liked the in-your-faceness of saying "my wife" to straight people. Now, as the world often saw me, I was one of those straight people, and I was doing everything I could to fight that perception.

When I was younger, my father, I think, struggled for the appropriate words for us; he didn't call Suzy my girlfriend or "my friend" but eventually settled on calling her my "co-pilot." Perhaps the phrase protected him from confronting my sexuality or from using the wrong lingo, since I'd never given him the language to use to describe my life. Either way, and as is often the case with my dad, without realizing it he gave me a great gift: a word that clearly defined what Jacob meant to me but didn't have the veneer of heterosexuality.

In the many years since Jacob first began his transition, I've come to embrace "husband" much more easily than I could during those early months, but I still use co-pilot frequently in front of a variety of audiences because it does perfectly define the role Jacob has played in my life without bogging listeners down with gender preconceptions. He frequently uses the term co-conspirator, which works well too.

Once people know Jacob and me, they understand our lives; until then, I like being able to emphasize his unending importance to me.

In life's journey, he's the only co-pilot I want, and it's not because of what is or isn't in his pants. It's because of what's in his heart.

CHAPTER NINE

SHUNNED

JACOB (SUZY)

My inner critic is occasionally eloquent, often incomprehensible, but never silent. It hasn't won me a lot of friends. My impulsive speaking out—my need to climb up on soapboxes—also caused a trans-men Listserv to ban me.

It was the first year of my transition and I visited the electronic bulletin board often. It was my first real source of contact with other trans guys, and while I didn't post very often, it was nice to read what other guys like me were going through and feeling. But it didn't take long before I started to wonder if these guys really were like me.

First someone posted a reprint of "Top 10 Dating Mistakes Men Make," by David DeAngelo, whose credentials apparently come from the five years he claims he spent reading "everything about men and women dating." His website seems to be a marketing vehicle for his e-book. Many of these tips are incomplete, leaving the real meat of the advice for those who pay for the answer. He offers to show readers "The difference between how men and women think about dating—and why most women want to keep you from being successful."

DeAngelo's sexist comments and the lack of context provided by the person who posted the piece offended me. I wrote a long criticism of the piece and ended with the question, "Am I the only feminist on this list?"

Most on-list responses accused me of lacking a sense of humor or not being a real guy's guy. A couple of people sent me off-list replies to assure me I wasn't the only feminist FTM guy out there.

Then the list administrator offered to make copies of *TransParent*—a documentary about transgender people who were also parents, by Jules Rosskam—for anyone who wanted to see it. The film had yet to be released on DVD; in fact it hadn't even been picked up by a distributor and had just opened at several LGBTQ film festivals. As one of the trans men featured in the film, he'd received a copy of the as-yet-unreleased DVD.

Having spent years in the world of publishing and entertainment, I was profoundly aware of the fact that many people involved in LGBTQ projects struggle for financial support to continue their important work. Considering how hard it is for queer filmmakers to find funding, especially when making independent films about transgender people, it seemed utterly wrong for this person to deny the filmmaker potential income. Worse, in the conversations that followed, the Listserv administrator kept insisting on "correcting" anyone who referred to the filmmaker as a fellow trans guy.

Instead, the list administrator dismissed the filmmaker as "whatsername" and said, "Meeting her, I thought she was FtM or something like that but in correspondence since, it was clear she is a she." He also called Rosskam "a (very masculine-looking) dyke who finds FtMs hot" and "this guy [who] is not FtM but something other, third gender or whatever."

I joined a number of other list members in writing to object to both the piracy and gender-identity issues. Many trans people go through periods during which they try on different identities, so their identification with, say, the term "FTM" might come and go. But that shouldn't mean we reject them as not being authentically trans. More importantly, we should allow people to identify the way they want to. At the time I'd recently interviewed Rosskam for my TransNation column. Speaking with me he'd clearly identified as a trans guy, not a lesbian.

I also found it was particularly troubling that the list administrator insisted on using female pronouns as a way of denigrating Rosskam. By calling the filmmaker a woman and/or a dyke, the list administrator was trying to dismiss Rosskam as not an FTM, not "one of us."

I'm not sure if it played a part in the way this went down, but I later learned that the Listserv owner had allegedly asked Rosskam to cut him from the film because he'd had second thoughts about its potential to out him.

Anyway, I thought Rosskam should be aware of the postings and the fact that someone was giving away his film, so I sent him a heads-up. Then I went off-line for the weekend. And when I returned I discovered that I'd inadvertently unleashed a maelstrom of toxic outbursts on the Listserv.

The list owner had been on a witch hunt to root out the source of what he called a "leak." He even accused several list moderators of being the ones to "betray" him by informing Rosskam about the conversations in question and took the extreme step of disbanding the moderators' group.

I quickly "confessed" and apologized for the problems I'd caused. The apology never made it on to the Listserv, but the administrator obviously read it, as I was immediately and permanently banished from the community.

I know privacy is critical to many LGBTQs, especially those who aren't out—who perhaps don't have the luxury of being out. If by following my conscience I broke that trust, I'm willing to pay the consequences.

But it does sadden me that one of the biggest online communities for trans guys is run like a dictatorship by a sexist and vengeful administrator. When FTM role models provide a forum where it's okay to question a person's gender-identity and denigrate women, what does that teach trans men who're just coming out? When our role models aren't out themselves, does that discourage the next generation from proudly embracing their transgender identities? When dissenting voices are censored before they can even raise criticisms, how will our community ever grow more tolerant?

Still it's kind of ironic that the very trans guys who accused other trans guys of less-than-masculine behavior shunned me. At its core, shunning is about relationships and the belief that severing relationships is the most painful form of punishment available. For that reason—and because it's typically a nonviolent resolution of conflict—sociologists have labeled shunning a more feminine tactic.

DIANE

We left the San Francisco Bay Area and moved to Portland, another city I'll always adore. I kept my job at *Curve*. I'd talked Franco into letting me try something I'd always wanted to do: living outside the Bay Area while continuing to run the magazine. So I flew back and forth between San Francisco and Portland every few weeks, always arriving in San Francisco in time for production of the magazine. I had the best of both worlds. The low cost of living and wonderful friends I'd made in Portland complemented the modernism and liberalism and good friends I'd made in San Francisco. Most importantly, I had the job I loved, even if I often was too tired to do it justice. I felt worldly and important from the constant travel, though I did tire of leaving my family behind and waking up in random hotel rooms, never remembering at first where I was.

That first year in Portland I joined the board of directors of the feminist pop-culture media company that produces *Bitch* magazine, and I started a big-girl burlesque dance troupe called Bang Bang Betty's Big Beautiful Bombshells (or B6, as promoters called it). I was Bang Bang Betty, and I loved it. Portland was friendly and slow, and everything was cheap by comparison. But it also had a literary and cultural bent, and the city was home to several LGBTQ luminaries, from the band Gossip to filmmaker Gus Van Sant and author Chuck Palahniuk.

Portland was the big city we'd traveled to as teens in high school, annual summer pilgrimages where I got to buy my school clothes and get a fancy haircut. So living there suddenly felt as close to Idaho as I could get, and I started thinking about permanent roots again.

CHAPTER TEN

TRANSNATION

JACOB (SUZY)

In an interview, Jennifer Finney Boylan, the author of the transition memoir *She's Not There*, once shared with me a piece of advice she'd received about not becoming a "professional transsexual." A friend had suggested to Boylan that those who remain part of the transgender community haven't successfully transitioned, because to be successful the trans person must *become* their preferred sex. "Introduce yourself as a woman," the friend recommended to her. "Not a transsexual."

I understand the argument and I've certainly heard it before, on both sides of the gender divide. It has to do with how one identifies after transition (pretending for a moment that transition has distinct start and end points—something that simply isn't true for many trans or genderqueer people). A lot of MTF and FTMs both identify not as trans but as women and men respectively. When I interviewed pro golfer Mianne Bagger for *Bitch* magazine, she told me about her "transsexual past." And I can personally attest to the simple joy and utter privilege of *passing*.

But I've spent so many years as an openly lesbian writer that being completely in the closet or being "stealth" in my professional life has never appealed to me. (Nor would it have been possible since I am married to Diane.)

So, soon after I came out, I became a professional trans person. I'd begun to increase my freelance writing and was blogging for *Curve* about my transition—Butch To Boy—but found I quickly grew bored with writing about myself. I'd also noticed a dearth of coverage of trans issues in the media, even in LGBTQ publications and websites.

In late 2005, I pitched the idea of a new column, TransNation, to the *San Francisco Bay Times*. Unlike many columns that are opinion pieces, this would be a space where I would present profiles of trans, genderqueer, and other gender-variant folks. Each week I interviewed another person, and that gave me an added bonus.

I was still pretty disabled from the back injury I'd received from trying to manhandle a huge trailer when I was a ranger and still spent most of my time alone at home, lying on the floor with my laptop propped on my knees. So I didn't get out a lot.

Interviewing people from my new community helped me connect with that community and begin to understand its true diversity and depth. At the time, interest in the trans community was also increasing and, with it, came a growing demand for media coverage. But at the same time, LGBTQ publications were and are still struggling against financial constraints that make it difficult for them to add that coverage themselves.

TransNation was the perfect solution for them. I did the work and provided weekly content, and publications paid me a small per-column fee. The column started in *Bay Times* (which ran every column I wrote), but after I began self-syndicating it soon appeared in LGBTQ publications from San Francisco to New York and on the Web.

I rarely wrote about my subjects' actual transition; I didn't ask what surgeries they'd had or the difficulties they had to face growing up gender variant. I asked about their work, their identities, their experience with discrimination, and what they wanted LGBTQ readers to know about them.

I tried to let my subjects speak for themselves—even when that meant setting my personal opinions aside. I showcased the diversity of the trans community, talking to folks from all walks of life, including those whose voices frequently went unheard, such as trans people who identified as straight and those who were adamant about not being a part of the LGBTQ community.

During TransNation's tenure, I interviewed some of the most renowned trans people in the world—from actresses like Candis Cayne (from ABC's *Sexy Dirty Money*) and Calpernia Addams, to playwrights Kate Bornstein and Scott Turner Schofield; authors Max Wolf Valerio and Jamison Green, to musicians like Lucas Silveira, Katastrophe, Shawna Virago, and Joshua Klipp, to porn star Buck Angel, dancer Sean Dorsey, and former Las Vegas showgirl Jahna Steele; and literally dozens of other activists, politicians, artists, scholars, athletes, and filmmakers. I still feel incredibly honored to have spoken with so many remarkable individuals who just happened to be differently gendered.

After interviewing and profiling over a hundred and fifty trans people in the weekly column, I retired TransNation in early 2009. Although I was burned out, it was difficult in some ways to let the column go, and I got some flak from the trans community for doing so. After all, I'd been one of the few trans writers published in these LGBTQ publications, and they feared coverage of trans issues would decline if I was no longer providing the content.

DIANE

I probably pushed Jacob to create TransNation, and to talk in print about trans issues, as much as he pushed himself. I've always wanted to both introduce lesbians to the outside world and to look at the mainstream world from a lesbian lens. After Jacob's transition, my mission grew to include transgender issues and people as well as those related to bisexual, queer, and genderqueer people—really the margins of our LGBTQ. And because Jacob could no longer be a park ranger, probably the first job I had seen him truly love rather than be alternately thrilled with and frustrated by, delving into freelance writing seemed a smart move. It gave him something to do, let him dive into what it meant to be a trans man, and sort of gave himself and the world a short course on the oh so many ways that transgender people could live, love, work, and identify.

Ironically, I had frustrations too. I had always wanted my own column, but my role as a magazine editor never gave me the time to pursue that option (plus magazines have non-compete clauses that prevent me from writing about LGBTQ issues for other media outlets). I think a tiny part of me was living vicariously through him during the time he wrote the column, and because very frequently "success" is all I see at the end of a tunnel, I probably pushed him hard to keep developing a wider audience, find more publications, became a known authority on trans issues.

I was both envious at times and frustrated by how easily things would come to him and how little he seemed to realize the great privilege writing this column afforded him. I had literally been writing for publications since I was a teenager and had really put in my time before I found success (and earned any money), but Jacob sort of waltzed right into it and became published. He would sometimes not seem to realize what a swift accomplishment he had earned, getting syndicated, being posted in publications around the country, and having editors call him up with assignments rather than having to pitch them cold. Most of the time I was just exceedingly proud, though, and bragged to everyone about him and his work. What he was doing opened my eyes a bit, too, and I wouldn't be the trans advocate I am today without having sort of gotten that crash course in how to talk about, and to, transgender people, and what issues are really key to their lives today. I learned the language, something few people have, and try to make sure I do trans people justice in my work today.

CHAPTER ELEVEN

BEING MARRIED TO A LESBIAN DOESN'T MAKE ME LESS OF A MAN

JACOB (SUZY)

In the summer of 2013—just as the Supreme Court decided that a key section of the Defense of Marriage Act is unconstitutional and Proposition 8 should be struck down—a trans guy stirred up a flurry of comments on Facebook by stating unequivocally that a lesbian cannot *be* a lesbian and date a trans man. Soon afterward, he deleted his post, replacing it with the following statement:

I'm deleting my last status do [sic] to the fact that it's blowing up my phone...I personally would NEVER be with someone who said they were a lesbian. Sorry if I offended anyone. I personally just don't understand how that works when in today's society, [a] 'lesbian' is a woman who dates women. I feel like when she does that and keeps the label she is telling society that she sees her partner as a woman. I do not know ANY women in my life that would be okay marrying a man or dating a man that tells everyone he is gay.

While thousands celebrated the Supreme Court's ruling with the widely repeated phrase "Love Is Love," the Facebook post was a stark reminder that, even within the LGBTQ community, many people do not truly believe that all love is equal.

The post's author wasn't the first person to express this idea, nor is he the only trans person to believe it. One night in 2008, I was hosting my radio show, *Gender Blender*, on Portland, Oregon's KBOO (90.7 FM) when my co-host—a trans woman—asked whether I ever worried that Diane couldn't see me as a *real* man.

Diane was a guest on the show, sitting in the studio with us, so close I felt her flinch at the question.

Since that evening we've heard the question many times. It seems one of the most difficult things for other people to understand about our relationship. After all, my wife, Diane, not only continued to identify as a lesbian after my transition, but she also continued to run the world's largest lesbian publication for several years *after* I became a man. While some lesbians certainly questioned her right to maintain her lesbian credentials and represent the lesbian community in the media, I fielded far more questions from other trans folk about Diane's capacity to see and love me as a "real" man.

For many trans men, the love of a lesbian is suspect compared to the love of a straight woman or a gay man. Likewise, for many trans women, the love of a straight woman is suspect compared to the love of a straight man or a lesbian. And for many trans people of any gender or sexual orientation, the love of a bisexual (man or woman) is also suspect.

Trans people worry about being seen for who they are and being seen as "real." They fear that some attractions and some love can only happen if the other person isn't seeing them authentically. In other words, in the view of some trans men, a lesbian-identified woman wouldn't be with a trans man if she actually saw him *as* a man.

For trans men who were with their partner before transitioning, the fear is a little more complex and revolves around this question: "After being in an intimate relationship in which you saw my naked body and you looked upon me as a female, can you really, truly see me as the male I now identify as?"

Did Geppetto still see the toy he'd carved after Pinocchio was made into a *real* boy? Or had he always seen the real boy hiding beneath Pinocchio's wooden features?

Even when our partners assure us they really *do* see us—the *real* us—we often have a hard time believing them. Particularly if our partners continue to retain their own pre-transition identities.

But is the partner of someone who goes through a gender transition required to alter their own self-identification? Is your sexual orientation truly determined by the shape of your partner's genitalia? If so, how should partners of trans people who haven't undergone genital surgery identify? Or does your partner's gender identity or gender expression determine how you should identify?

I want to ask other trans people, "What makes our right to self-identify sacrosanct, while our partners must have their identities determined for them based on particular attributes not about themselves, but about us?" If a straight woman is married to a man and that man transitions to a woman, then we seem to want to force them into a gay relationship and require them to identify as lesbians. Likewise, when—after nearly fifteen years as part of a lesbian couple—I transitioned, people seemed to believe that Diane was required to alter her identity, because, the theory goes, she couldn't remain a lesbian while continuing to be with me.

I find it almost offensive that this line of argument originates so frequently from trans individuals. Trans people have often argued, almost vehemently, that it doesn't matter what we look like physically, it doesn't matter what other people think, it doesn't matter what style of clothing we wear, it doesn't matter if our voices have changed or if we've undergone surgery or if we started hormone treatment—the only thing that matters is how we identify.

Once I verbalize my gender identity, I expect to be taken at my word. If I say I'm a man, I expect you to accept me as a man.

I could be wearing a dress, I could look like Miss America, and if I say I'm really a man, then you're supposed to accept that I am.

So it's almost incomprehensible to me that we as a community or that individuals who identify as trans wouldn't use the same logic when it comes to other people's identities. It's not our place to identify someone else as a lesbian or as a straight person or as a bisexual person. It's completely up to them to decide and verbalize what their sexual orientation is.

This double standard is offensive. We can't demand the freedom of self-identification for ourselves and then not allow other people that same right. Like everyone else, Diane has the right to choose her own identities and to proclaim, "This is who I am," and be taken at her word.

I dislike for members of any minority to take it upon themselves to police their communities and determine who has the right to belong. When I first came out as trans, the Listserv moderator who suggested that some people weren't really trans men because they were too feminine offended me. I've seen this kind of policing everywhere I've lived, and especially on the Internet, where people are more unabashed in sharing their feelings.

It would be bad enough if the lesbian community insisted upon strict qualifications for a lesbian identity. But when someone outside that community suggests that they have a better idea of what components are essential to that identity, it's even more offensive.

It's as though the poster on Facebook who couldn't understand how a true lesbian could continue her relationship with a FTM was suggesting that by remaining in my long-term relationship with a woman who doesn't identify as straight, I'm less of a man than if I'd broken up with her and then insisted on only dating women who are straight or men who are gay.

For many trans men, it *is* a particular turn-on for straight women or gay men to find them attractive; it somehow validates their masculinity, somehow validates their self-image as a man. But it also suggests that only straight women and gay men have the visual acuity to see and correctly identify maleness in the world. Conversely, this would seem to indicate that only straight men and lesbians can correctly identify women and femaleness in the world. I just can't find anything to confirm or validate this kind of assumption.

The question of realness and whether I'm seen or not seen by my partner is also at the heart of my response to another query that I frequently receive when someone first discovers that I didn't transition until I was almost forty years old. People want to know why it took me so long to come out as transgender.

Diane was one of the major reasons I didn't feel it necessary to declare my trans gender earlier. She's always seen the "real me." Maybe she and I didn't initially understand that those aspects of the "real me" demonstrated that I was more appropriately identified as a trans man than as a lesbian, but she always saw my true essence. Whether you want to call it a soul or something else, Diane saw the real me, and she recognized and validated my masculinity in a way that allowed me to exist in the world in a female body without going crazy.

While I never felt entirely comfortable in my skin, with Diane I had long periods of time where I could forget that my external self didn't reflect my internal truth—until I passed a mirror or had some other reminder of my female-bodiedness. She saw and validated and loved me even when my body was misrepresenting me and rendering me invisible to the rest of the world. So why should I now think that Diane has become blind to my truth, post-transition? Why would I think that now that the rest of the world can see my maleness, she would suddenly see femaleness instead?

This doesn't mean that our transition as a couple was never a struggle. Of course it was. But part of that struggle comes not from the inherent issues that arise in such a life-changing event. Part of it comes from the fact that other people project their concerns, prejudices, and issues upon transitioning couples. When we first announced my new trans identity and told others I'd be transitioning from female to male, a surprising number of our closest friends and family members expressed their utter certainty that we wouldn't survive as a couple because "Diane is a lesbian."

One of the milestones about achieving true marriage equality will be in gaining validation of same-sex relationships on par with their straight counterparts. Even our own community hasn't always done a great job of supporting, validating, and helping to maintain long-term LGBTQ relationships. This is changing dramatically, of course, at least for same-sex couples.

But for many trans people, coming out still carries at the very least the fear that their relationship will end. Others expect it, and you expect it, whether you're coming from a queer or a straight relationship. Some part of this anticipation is internalized, but other people make it very clear that they foresee that you will break up because one of you is transitioning. No one tells you at that point that "love is love."

So as we celebrate the Supreme Court victories and herald an age of marriage equality, let's not forget that some relationships in our community are still fighting for validation. In addition to trans people, I'd say that many bisexuals are also still struggling for the greater society, and the LGBTQ community specifically, to recognize their relationships as having the same validity and value as anyone else's.

Although I believe wholeheartedly that Diane has seen the real me throughout our relationship, I also acknowledge that I've become a different person because of hormone therapy. Testosterone has made me into a different person, and this naturally puts unusual stresses on our relationship. Diane has had to adjust to these differences, to the way testosterone has altered my personality and my communication styles, but I still believe that she sees the "real me."

In fact, I know she now truly sees me as a man, in a way she did not before my transition. Not only does she tell me that she does, but she demonstrates it, dozens of times throughout the day. Sometimes it is in very subtle, nearly imperceptible cues. And other times, in ways that are blatant (and often unintentionally

hilarious), she demonstrates just how far the belief in my manhood
has penetrated into her subconscious.

❖

I've always known I'm having a high pain day when I'm at
the supermarket and women rush to my assistance. I don't mean
that they just hold the door for me, although that's already a sign
of something.

In our society women don't typically hold the door for men,
and men don't usually hold the door for other men, but both men
and women hold the door for the disabled. And—at least on my
high pain days—they hold the door for me.

But when I'm really having a tough day and feeling crippled
by pain, women always seem to know. They don't ask if I need or
want assistance.

They say things like, "You poor thing. Let me help."

And then they just take over. Total strangers will rush up and
push my cart, or pull down a box of cereal, or unload my things
onto the cashier's treadmill, or offer to carry bags to my car.

One day, I came home from grocery shopping and related my
latest such experience to Diane.

"Oh, my God," she replied. "How *emasculating*!"

I think my mouth gaped open.

What the—? I couldn't believe the words had come from
Diane's mouth.

Emasculating? We're feminists, for God sake. Wasn't that
supposed to mean we didn't believe in emasculation? I mean, isn't
emasculation the same as feminization or loss of masculinity?
How could that be offensive to a feminist? Isn't the whole threat
of being emasculated based on men's fear of being emotionally
castrated or otherwise feminized in some way?

I don't fear being treated the way women are treated. Not
really. I mean, I want to be recognized as a man, and I don't want
someone to treat me like less of a man *because* I'm trans. That

doesn't mean I don't still want to end gender discrimination and unequal compensation (I can't believe women still earn seventy-five cents for every dollar a bio guy makes).

But people have treated me like a woman most of my life, and not being seen as a strong, able-bodied stud isn't a blow to my masculinity or sense of self. I'm not muscle-bound, 100 percent able-bodied, or a he-man. I'm a shy, skinny, differently abled, bespectacled metrosexual geek who may know how to give his car an oil change but still prefers to pay someone else to do it. In a world of superhero comics I'd be the nerdy "before" picture, not the hulking post-transition hero.

Did I even have enough masculinity for someone to strip away? Could I even be emasculated?

As much as I still endlessly poke fun at Diane when she reveals unconscious and embarrassingly unfeminist, stereotypical gender expectations, it's exactly such knee-jerk reactions that prove beyond a reasonable doubt that Diane sees me as just another bio guy.

She's gotten mad at me for not being a gentleman, for not holding the door open for other women or not waiting for her to step out of an elevator before me. She even forgets that I haven't been a man all my life.

One night we were watching television and a commercial came on, revealing dire statistics about the number of men who die each year, basically because they're too embarrassed to get a prostate exam.

Diane turned to me with utter seriousness and concern and asked, "Have you had a prostate exam?"

I shook my head.

"Oh, my God, Jacob. You need to have one."

I laughed.

"It's not funny," she said. "We're getting older, and I don't want you dying of prostate cancer."

I told her, "That's not going to happen, honey."

"Oh, yeah?"

"Yeah."

As someone who was born female-bodied, I don't even have a prostate.

Diane knows this. But she's so accepted my maleness that she forgot I was different from other men. She's accepted this, not just in principle, but in the deepest parts of her subconscious mind. She's accepted my maleness not as something artificial or created but as utterly natural and all-encompassing.

So I know that Diane sees me as a man. If she can continue to see herself as a lesbian, even though she's married to a man, who am I to dissuade her? After all, I continue to see myself as part of the LGBTQ community even though I'm a man in a relationship with a woman. Diane continues to identify as queer, as a lesbian, sometimes clarifying her status by saying perhaps she's a bisexual-identified lesbian or as a lesbian-identified bisexual. Either way, together, we continue to identify as a queer couple. And none of this makes me any less of a man.

DIANE

When I was a kid, I had a relative with the best porn stash I'd ever seen. Mostly *Playboy* magazines, it was about four feet high, stacked row after row in a wall-size closet with rolling doors. In the pre-Internet, pre-home-video days, people (usually men) kept their erotica at home, in the back of a closet or on top of a cabinet, where it was safely contained and away from small developing minds. We kids were supposed to stay out of that closet, but when I could, I would sneak in and furtively ogle the beautiful women of *Playboy* (who I wanted to both be and do) and the graphic sex acts in *Swedish Erotica*.

It was there, in the back of one of the magazines in a small advertisement, that I saw my first transgender person, and before I came out as a lesbian and then as a feminist, before I learned that this type of advertising is highly derogatory to trans women because it equates all trans women with sex work and fetishizes trans women who are pre- or non-operative, before I knew all that, I was fascinated. I was attracted to the dichotomy I saw, the mix of feminine and masculine qualities in the same person.

That's the earliest I remember being attracted to both masculine and feminine qualities, but it's by far not the last. In high school in the 1980s, I loved the boys who wore eyeliner and the girls who could rope cattle, even though I dated neither. I thought Dolly Parton was perfect, even though she was mocked as over the top. (The same would be true in the 1990s of Anna Nicole Smith, one of the sexiest women I've ever seen.)

I've always wanted to *be* Anna Nicole or Heather Locklear, but as soon as I was aware of my sexual orientation, I've always wanted to have sex with butch, or masculine, women. Their energy, their sex appeal, their strength is something that just makes me weak in the knees. I'm not much of a starfucker. I always say journalists can't afford to be. We interview celebrities, and it's bad for our careers to be crushed out on them.

But throughout the 1990s, I made a serious exception for k.d. lang. She'd worn skirts and glasses in her earliest performances and I loved her weird quirkiness then, but once she ditched all that for men's suits and full-on butch swagger I didn't consider many celesbians more attractive, more wanted, than k.d. in her heyday.

When Jacob was still Suzy, he had that sweet butchness I adored—masculine, unformed, someone for whom femininity was uncomfortable. Her transformation as a butch started out small. When we met she was wearing khaki shorts (khaki is sexual repellent) and a pink protest T-shirt, but I could see she was itching to break out of this faux androgynous uniform she'd picked up during women's studies at college.

From the outside, it may look like I "made" her more butch, but it's simply not true. If anything, I just gave her permission, many times along the way, to become who she (and eventually he) wanted to be. Within our first few months together, she had bought a nice men's suit and cut her hair in a slightly longer version of the classic crew cut. We got our first couple's photo together that year, and Suzy, wearing that suit and some aviator glasses, is beaming. I don't think she'd ever had a girlfriend before who gave her permission to just become, just evolve, in whatever direction she wanted. Even now, that's one of Jacob's favorite photos of us.

For me, I had to evolve and adapt along the way too. It helped that I didn't find that androgynous woman very attractive. In fact, the day we met at Idaho's second gay pride parade, she seemed innocuous, young, disinterested even. A few weeks later we met again after she had borrowed clothes from a male friend, and I felt like I was meeting an entirely different person. The outfit seemed to bring out something different in her, something especially alluring: a brooding, butchy cynic with a comical flirtiness that just clicked with me.

We engaged in a lot of tipsy flirtation, some talk about how many letters in the alphabet our sexual conquests would cover, and essentially traded sexual barbs all night. I wanted her badly, and the next day I sent her a card that said, "I'd like to help you with that alphabet. I can supply D, L, and A (my initials). I'll be there for Halloween. Be prepared."

From that day forward, I saw the masculine person inside, and I've loved, and lusted after, it ever since.

Now though, I've been thinking more about the idea that one can be attracted to transgender men (or women) in part because of their transness, not (as mainstream culture seems to think) in spite of it. There's a lot of backlash when I say I think I'm now attracted to trans men, not cisgender men, because I do see something special, something better, there.

In 2013, a well-known DJ, Mister Cee, a renowned figure in urban music, got trans-shamed for soliciting a person he thought was a female trans sex worker. He resigned, and then his boss talked him into coming back. (After all, this is the guy who introduced the world to Notorious B.I.G.) He's come out about his orientation. He's a man attracted to trans women and cross-dressers. And yes, he hires sex workers who fit into these categories. (He's also agreed to get therapy, perhaps because of his predilection for hired hands, but that's another story.) After Mister Cee was outed I realized how much men are shamed for being attracted to or loving trans women.

"We, as a society, have not created a space for men to openly express their desire to be with trans women," author Janet Mock writes in her blog. "Instead, we shame men who have this desire, from the boyfriends, cheaters, and 'chasers' to the 'trade,' clients, and pornography admirers. We tell men to keep their attraction to trans women secret, to limit it to the Internet, frame it as a passing fetish or transaction. In effect, we're telling trans women that they are only deserving of secret interactions with men, further demeaning and stigmatizing trans women."

Mock says she's witnessed numerous so-called scandals, like those of Mister Cee, Eddie Murphy, and LL Cool J, "where passing interactions with trans women spawn hundreds of headlines, particularly for a man with fame and social capital." She asks, "When a man can be shamed merely for interacting with a trans woman—whether it be through a photograph, a sex tape or correspondences—what does this say about how society views trans women? More important, what does this do to trans women?"

The answer is plenty, and it's not good. But I'm thinking now about what it does to these admirers—the boyfriends and girlfriends, husband and wives of trans people. I feel a bit like Mister Cee some days, in that I maybe am reluctantly clinging to a label that doesn't fit, but perhaps *no* label fits. He feels straight, and he's attracted to women, which I say makes him straight; but the fact that he's attracted to women who sometimes still have male genitalia confuses people who need their binaries and bodies to be clearly delineated.

I came out as bisexual twenty-six years ago, then as queer a year later (and I still love and defend that term because I use it today as does Jacob, even though he is only attracted to women). When I was working at lesbian magazines I started using the term *lesbian* because those were the women with whom I was most closely aligned, devoted to even, and to whom I was attracted. Then, eight years ago, when my wife decided to come out as my husband, I was forced to reevaluate what any of these terms mean. I still use many interchangeably (lesbian-identified bisexual, queer, lesbian, bisexual-identified lesbian, and so on).

I'm, well, somewhere else now.

I've found myself in the last couple of years becoming more and more attracted to trans men. Not *all* men. Just trans men. There's something about transgender men I find exceptionally attractive both physically and mentally, especially those who were acculturated as lesbian feminists. I know some trans guys—like T Cooper, who has written about why dating a lesbian isn't as validating as dating a straight woman—find this idea offensive. And few lesbians I know understand how one can be attracted to trans men and not be straight. I don't know; sometimes trans men exude a beauty that I'm drawn to, like the dozens of lesbians before them.

I still *feel* like a lesbian—after nearly three decades of identifying as such, how could I not—but I still remember the backlash that followed JoAnn Loulan, the author of the definitive book on female relationships, *Lesbian Sex*, after she fell in love with a man, or Holly Near, when she did the same. I'm always afraid that'll happen to me, so I'm a bit afraid to say, well, maybe, just maybe there's something inside me that's interested in men now too.

Is it a case of the cart following the horse? Did loving Jacob eventually change my identity? Is being bisexual such a stigmatized identity that I'm afraid to claim it (and lose my lesbian cred)? Look, I'm not the only queer woman who's attracted to both women and trans men; Michelle Tea and Beth Ditto have both had well-known relationships with both.

What I do know, what is my baseline through all this, is that I love Jacob, and have since we met in 1991. I've always found him one of the most attractive people I've ever seen. And while I mourned the woman he was as she was cast away, I embraced who he became on the outside so readily because, for the most part, the person on the inside didn't fundamentally change. There has been a masculine person in that body since we met; that person has just evolved, morphed, adapted, and changed in ways that are, in large part, purely cosmetic. In the duration of our relationship, I've gained and lost nearly 200 pounds, gained wrinkles, lost sight, and gone from a brunette rockabilly chick to a blond cardigan-wearing bookworm. We all change. His just involved his genitals too.

Chapter Twelve

The Question of Realness

JACOB (SUZY)

Still, the question of realness lingers. It's sort like a persistent fog—ghostlike, the kind of thing you can't see head-on, but only from the corner of your eye. (Apparently some biological basis for this exists. Humans have more rods—or is it cones?—on the side of our eyes so we see certain things better peripherally.)

People don't usually address the realness of my masculinity straight out, but sometimes it's there swimming below the surface like a double entendre hinting at a word's true meaning.

People want to know what my genitalia look like. They want to know if I'm an innie or an outtie, as though there are only two options. As though knowing the answer would reveal something essential about me, or about Diane, or about our relationship.

It's not just the gender-ignorant that ask me which surgeries I've had. Even other trans people want to know. Before she would answer any of my questions, one prominent MTF writer I interviewed for TransNation demanded to talk about the medical interventions I'd had. She wanted to know if I was "done."

Some trans folk, especially some middle-class trans women—who've had access to the best surgeries available—see the transition process as a finite experience, one that occurs over a specific period of time. You start on one side visibly male/female, then you go through counseling, hormone treatments, and surgery, and you end up on the other side passing as female/male. The transition is then over; you may even no longer consider yourself trans, because you're "done." You're now fully a woman/man.

For many others, especially trans men and those of limited economic resources, transition isn't a distinct day or year. It's a process, one that can take a long time: years, decades, or the rest of our lives.

It's been years since my distinct dates, and in some ways I do feel "done." I just feel like I'm me, Jacob, a dude who goes through his day like any other dude. But in other ways, for me, being "done" would be akin to being dead. I don't know if I'll stop transitioning until I die. I certainly expect to continue changing, growing, becoming until death ends that process. Actually, I'll continue after death—decomposing, transitioning to yet another state of being.

Essentially, the question is, what makes someone the sex that they are. What makes a man a man? Is it a penis? A certain level of testosterone? XY chromosomes? Certain experiences? Behaviors? Values?

I'm an XX boy. My chromosomes still say I'm female, but my hormone levels and appearance indicate that I'm male. Am I a real man? If a man loses his penis to accident or disease does he cease to be a man?

If I haven't had bottom surgery, does that mean I'm not a man, but if I've had the surgery I am one? Is it having the money or access to medical care that determines whether or not I'm real?

Diane and I decided a few years ago to be vague about which surgeries I've undergone and what exactly my private parts look like. We think it's a personal, private matter what our genitals look like. We assume most people share that belief, that most people don't want to drop trou just to appease curious onlookers. When people ask about my penis, Diane often says, "Show me yours and I'll show you mine." Or if a man is asking her about it, she'll suggest they talk about his wife's vagina too.

Because race, gender, and socio-economic factors also play major roles in the kind of surgeries and resultant genitalia that trans folk have access to, it's not fair if we allow only those who haven't had access to surgery to bear the brunt of the societal pressures that arise when you won't publicly describe your surgeries and private parts.

Before the current wave of marriage equality, the only people who used the term "partner" were gay and lesbian couples unable to marry, so just using the term opened you up for discrimination. Now plenty of people do, and it takes away the marginalization that the word holds. When actor Philip Seymour Hoffman died, many media reports referenced his long-time female partner.

If the only people who put their foot down about protecting their right to privacy are the ones who *haven't* had surgery, we acquiesce to both the invasion of privacy and the hierarchy that grants more acceptance to those who've undergone the surgeries that most make them conform to societal expectations of male and female physicality.

Because Diane and I don't answer the question directly, others like to assume for us one way or the other. Some have found comfort in the assumption that I haven't had bottom surgery, because for them it serves as some kind of explanation about why Diane and I have beaten the odds and stayed together. If my clothing hides female genitalia, these people are more comfortable accepting Diane as a lesbian and think it explains why she stays with me.

Presumably this means Diane can still be a lesbian if I haven't had surgery, but not if I have? What if I have a penis but haven't had my ovaries removed? These assumptions imply that "real" men need penises. Real women don't have penises; real men don't have vaginas or uteruses. If you believe this is true you need to read a good book on the sexual diversity in humans and discover how frequently children are born who don't fit neatly into nice, clean, distinct boxes of boys or girls. (First start: Google "intersex.")

On the other hand, when people assume I *have* undergone every possible surgery and upgrade, they sometimes ask Diane equally invasive questions like, "Don't you miss pussy?" (If people also assume we are non-monogamous, then they think that explains it as well. Clearly, they think, Diane must have sex with women on the side.)

Why does it matter what's under my clothes?

Non-trans people seem to fixate on trans people's genitals. This sort of reductive thinking leads to two central areas of concerns: the bathroom and the bedroom. The most frequent questions we get asked revolve around how we go to bathroom and how we have sex.

The fixation with my private parts really bothers me. Although I'm public about a lot of things in my life, I'm relatively shy about bodily functions—even in private. I don't like people to watch—or even hear—me go to bathroom. I have a very shy bladder. I often have to plug my ears so I can't hear other people and can pretend I'm in a cone of silence. I mean I literally stick my fingers in my ears in order to go to bathroom, even in the privacy of my own home. Even when I just need to pee, I kick Diane out of the room and turn on the fan.

I find questions about how I go to the bathroom (or have sex) to be very invasive. And there's something dehumanizing about reducing another person to a single body part. If you're going to reduce me to one, I would prefer it be my brain.

With that said, here's the full disclosure about how I go to the bathroom: I go to the bathroom by walking into a private or public facility, shutting the door, standing in front of or sitting down on a ceramic waste-disposal device, unzipping or lowering my pants, and tightening certain muscles (and allowing gravity to do its work) until my urine flows through my urethra or my solid waste is expelled from my bowels. Then I wipe, flush, wash my hands, and leave.

How do *you* go to the bathroom? Do you have some exotic, exciting method for expelling waste that differs dramatically from the above? Don't keep it to yourself. We're all waiting with bated breath.

Although both bath and bed rooms are considered private spaces in American homes, fears and concerns about bathrooms have been central to public discourse around accepting transgender coworkers in the workplace. The greatest trans-phobic fear-mongering tends to revolve around these questions and has often tried to depict public bathrooms as sites where trans perverts stalk sexual prey.

In fact, when it comes to trans women, some great feminist analysis has pointed out that the rhetoric reimagines the public bathroom not only as private space but as an extension of the (cisgender) female body and equates the entry of trans women as an unwanted invasion of that body. In other words, cisgender women complaining about trans women using the women's bathroom said they felt "violated" and "raped."

Even before I transitioned I had been confronted in and run out of women's bathrooms and even had security called on me when women mistook me for a man. Now, as a guy, I'm sort of lucky, because while cisgender women may police their restrooms, men do not. In fact, as other FTMs informed me when I first transitioned, most straight men are too homophobic to ever look at another man's junk.

Still, I know many trans men are very concerned about using public facilities because of the fear of having their gender-incongruent bodies discovered. They fear men will respond with violence and or rape. Of course, this fear has roots in reality: Brandon Teena, a trans man who was first raped and then later murdered, after his body incongruence was discovered. But trans women bear most of the brunt of transphobic violence and hate crimes.

A few trans activists confronted bathroom issues head-on by founding the organization Safe2Pee, with the mission of providing trans folk with a guide to gender neutral or otherwise trans-friendly restrooms that could be accessed by the general public. They created an app that was able to geo-tag locations and suddenly found they were being used by an unexpected demographic: moms searching for nearby family-friendly restrooms. Years later, a transgender coder, Teagan Widmer, invented an app called Refuge Restrooms, which is also about finding safe bathrooms for trans people.

In his recent work of nonfiction, *Real Man Adventures*, award-winning trans author T Cooper asked non-trans men if they would be comfortable sitting down to pee in a public bathroom. Although several men admitted sitting down at home, the majority said they would be uncomfortable doing so in public.

Personally, I've never had a negative interaction in a men's room. When I first came out I was concerned and bought a stand-to-pee device. It took a little maneuvering to get the device positioned correctly so I didn't have urine dripping down my leg. But no one ever looked at me differently.

Eventually, I stopped worrying about peeing in men's rooms.

The truth is, nowadays I mostly sit to pee, regardless of whether I'm at home or in public. The reason has very little to do with my gender transition and very much to do with my transition from able-bodied to disabled. First of all, a side effect of some of my medication is that I have trouble beginning a stream. Even when I feel like I have to pee this very second, when I get in position, nothing happens. I have stood/sat for nearly thirty minutes, alternating straining and relaxing all my muscles, before the first drop hits the bowl.

Secondly, I find standing in place very difficult. The pain in my left foot becomes unbearable, and I end up lifting it and standing, stork-like, on one foot. I often use a cane to keep my balance. But propping myself up on the cane leaves me with one less hand to maneuver, and even with the cane, the pain usually wins out and I give up and sit down.

Eventually I just stopped worrying about whether someone in the stall next to me might wonder why I'm not standing up when they can hear me urinating. I think most of us in the men's room just want to get in and do our business and get out.

❖

Although Diane is comfortable sharing the details about our sex life, I am rather inhibited and reserved when it comes to talking about sex. And I'm no exhibitionist. I don't like to be seen naked. I don't like to describe my genitals or share photos of them, not even via sext messages to my wife.

I don't like to describe my sex life in detail. I've never videotaped myself having sex. I can write sex scenes, but when it comes to reading those sections of our books aloud, I blush and stammer and want to disappear. I can't always enjoy depictions of other people having sex, because I get embarrassed (by and for them).

Straight people used to wonder how gay people could have sex. In fact, at one point in history, the very definition of sex itself precluded any notion of two women in bed. More recently, it wasn't uncommon for a straight man to ask a lesbian couple, "So, which one of you is the man?" demonstrating a worldview in which there are only penetrators and penetratees.

Of course, that worldview presupposes that straight people have only sex missionary style, gay men have only anal, and lesbians have only oral sex. (Bisexuals, as everyone knows, are all over the board.)

No matter how you personally identify, when was the last time you had a sexual experience where you conformed to those stereotypes? With more straight men (and women) experimenting with anal sex, with the use of toys, with the mainstreaming of oral (and anal) sex, with *Shades of Grey* and BDSM, with swingers and threesomes and jack-off parties—with all the diverse and wonderful ways humans have invented to have sex, there's something dehumanizing about assuming that trans people have a different kind of sex, that our genitals somehow preclude "normal" sexuality and drop us into a shadowy, perverse world so bizarre—and even threatening—that it must be separately categorized, must be studied, must be brought into public space for all the "normal" cisgender people to view and judge. It's like being in a freak show or in a zoo. It's like having your "mating rituals" on display for the voyeuristic entertainment of others.

How do I have sex? The same way you do.

I touch my partner's body. Our bodies touch each other. We kiss. We make out. We engage in foreplay. Sometimes we look at erotic imagery, sometimes we don't. Sometimes we experiment. We try different positions, but we have our favorites. We have objects made of silicone in our bedroom: sometimes we use them, sometimes we don't.

Sometimes we talk while we're having sex. Usually it's not about the bills. We both enjoy (giving and getting) oral pleasure, but neither of us is into butt stuff (not that there's anything wrong with it). Sometimes we have sex frequently; other times it feels like it's been forever. Sometimes one of us is more eager than the other. Sometimes we just cuddle. Sometimes I'm in too much pain to do anything but kiss. We rarely role-play any more (there's no one I'd rather she be), and (these days) we tend to prefer a good old bed to exotic locales. Usually our sex ends with multiple orgasms, but sometimes it doesn't. Sometimes we stop having sex because one of our adorable dogs has decided we're playing a fun game and ruins the moment. After twenty-three years, it's safe to assume we've tried almost everything in the bedroom, at least all but that which leaves serious bruises or causes bleeding.

The intimate details about our sex life, descriptions of our genitalia, and any agreements we have about the boundaries of our relationship aren't really anyone's business but our own. It's invasive, offensive even to ask such questions.

But I'm not the kind of guy who believes he owns his wife's body or should hold the only key to her chastity belt. As far as I'm concerned, Diane is free to have sex with another woman. She's free to have sex with another man. She's free to have sex with a trans guy, a trans woman, a genderqueer or intersex person. Diane can have sex with anyone she wants.

Unfortunately, saying we have an agreement or out-of-town rules or any other arrangement often elicits responses that Diane's no more comfortable with than assumptions of prudishness.

"Oh, that explains it," they say, maybe throwing in a wink for good measure, telling her they get it, now; now they understand how she can still identify as a lesbian while being married to a trans guy.

They've got it all wrong. Just because she has the freedom to be with others doesn't mean she chooses to. Now that I'm a guy she's not out having sex with other women, consoling her lesbian lust, every weekend.

And like any woman's, Diane's identity, sexual and otherwise, isn't tied up with me and mine. That being the case, Diane is a lesbian (or bi- or queer) because she identifies as one, and she'll remain a lesbian as long as she continues to identify as such, regardless of who she's actually sleeping with. And regardless of whether her partner's identity has changed.

Should a woman who's dedicated her twenty-five-year-career to serving the queer community no longer be allowed to do so because her lesbian partner now identifies as a trans man? Should her commitment to the lesbian community be in doubt while some celebrities need merely have kissed a girl for lesbians to claim her as one of their own for life?

A few detractors—including one close former friend in what felt like an enormous personal betrayal to Diane—have publicly questioned her right to edit *Curve* after I transitioned. She argued that a woman married to a man, albeit a trans man, was, by definition, *heterosexual* and therefore no longer qualified to run the nation's largest lesbian magazine.

So far those kind of contentions have been few and haven't had a serious, negative impact on Diane's career, but at times such comments wore on her, eating away at her confidence and her convictions until she was questioning if her critics were right, if she should just walk away from a career she loved because the woman she loved became a man she loved.

"What if they're right?" Diane texted me one night from Portland's Baghdad Theater, where she was staffing a table at the *Curve*-sponsored screening of *The L Word*. "What if I'm no longer a lesbian?"

I called her right away and asked what had brought this up tonight.

She said hundreds of cute lesbians were packed into the theater, but she wouldn't want to have sex with even one of them.

I asked her if she'd seen guys recently she was attracted to.

"No," she admitted, sounding worried. "Do you think I've lost interest in sex?"

I laughed. "All indications point to no. Maybe you just haven't found anyone else recently you'd rather have sex with than me?"

If we only want to have sex with each other, what does that make us? I like to say we're queer. But even more: we are married. And while we have agreements that allow for other experiences, we are, on the whole, monogamous. Monogamy isn't the loss of desire; it's just the channeling of desire, focusing it on one person.

Personally, I think Diane has blinders on when it comes to me and what she perceives as my more-attractive-than-anyone-else-ness, but who am I to complain? I'm just happy she still finds me attractive after all these years. I'm just thrilled she still desires my body after all the changes it's gone through.

I'm just glad I'm still her queerly beloved.

DIANE

I'm not shy. I can talk about sex at length. I'm a braggart, a reformed slut who's proud of her past. Though I no longer remember the names of many of the forty-five people I slept with before Jacob came around, I can probably recall the experiences I had with them. And save for one time, I've never had an experience I regret.

Jacob doesn't love it when I talk about sex though, at least as it relates to him. He was raised a good Catholic kid, and I think that sense of guilt and privacy stays forever with a person. His own sexuality has ebbed and flowed as we've gotten older, and I've mostly ridden the waves as they've come.

When we were younger we had toys galore, and sexy outfits and costumes, we could have sex anywhere without distraction—we once stopped off the road in a national forest and had sex on a log just barely out of sight of the road and loved it—and there was little you could do to keep my hands off him.

The year he was injured, he felt so bad both physically and emotionally we went without sex for an entire year. I didn't enjoy that year, and Jacob was quick to tell me he understood if I got my needs met elsewhere. I did, with my right hand and a small buzzing blue object. I missed sex that year and was thrilled when one day he was finally ready to have a go at it again.

Even now there is one gender stereotype we don't conform to: I'm usually the aggressor, the initiator. And I still desire him in a way I wouldn't expect of a couple who had been together more than two decades. He is still movie-star gorgeous at forty-five, and if he'd let me I'd fuck him every night.

But the transition from woman to man did change our sex lives in the beginning. I think because I was so cognizant then of helping him become a "man," something I kept thinking of as so distinctly different, that I went overboard in those early days. Here's one example: when I discovered that men's and women's shirts (never say blouse) buttoned on the opposite sides, I went through Jacob's closet and pulled out any shirt that buttoned on the wrong side and sent them to Goodwill. I was trying so hard to sort of help him succeed at manhood, that I forgot to think about simply the person he was. He didn't care which side his shirts buttoned, but I was sure it would somehow tip off other men that he had previously been a woman. All this, even though we were going on talk shows and doing interviews with newspapers, including *The New York Times*, talking about that very thing. It made little sense.

I think my desire to succeed has always been foisted on Jacob a bit (sometimes unfairly, but that's what you get when you marry me), and so when he announced his transition, I made it a goal to make it the best damn transition possible. He needed not just to be a man but to be the perfect man. And that meant my job was validating his manhood and his masculinity.

And so it was with sex. As a lesbian couple we had a lot of different types of sex. We used toys, enjoyed penetration, had a lot of oral sex (the receiving of which is quite frankly one of my favorite things in life). In the first few weeks of his manhood, his doctor and my therapist had both warned me that the new hormones he was taking would essentially push him through a second puberty. They would give him acne and make him incredibly horny.

"Imagine a fourteen-year-old boy," my shrink said.

"Maybe I'll finally match your sex drive," Jacob joked when I told him that.

The doctors were right. All the changes that he started going through—the hair growth on his face, his new muscles, the acne and oily skin, his voice deepening—it all started happening immediately. Even his smell, his body odor changed. Most importantly, he got that teenage sex drive.

And new things began to turn him on. You know that Sir Mix-A-Lot song "Baby Got Back," in which he sings about liking big butts? Well, Jacob could have taken that as an anthem. For about six months he wanted a lot of sex, and I was down with it.

Instead of doing a lot of our old same moves, I realized he was suddenly very interested in sex in which he could see my bottom. So I sort of planned and maneuvered every encounter in that direction, eschewing oral sex (at least receiving it) altogether for months because I so associated oral with lesbian sex. I wanted him to know I saw him as a man, I loved him as a man, and I wanted to have sex with him as a man (yes, even while proclaiming my lesbian identity; ours is a murky world).

Jacob was down with it for a few months, and then he withdrew a bit, seemed less interested, and after we talked I realized he was bored with this new routine, feeling penned in by this "heterosexual" sex, and it made me too realize that by trying to validate him as a man, I had sort of marginalized him even more. If I saw him as masculine before and masculine now, why couldn't he have any type of sex?

The answer of course is that he could. Any type of sex is queer, or straight, or whatever we are, whatever is in-between and blended, and remembering that has led to even deeper intimacy as we move from a lesbian couple to a male-female one.

CHAPTER THIRTEEN

WHAT HAPPENS IN VEGAS

DIANE

After several unsuccessful tries at artificial insemination (which involved nitrogen tanks, frozen sperm, pot holders, and sexless procreation attempts), I tried to get pregnant once more when I was forty. It was many years after a miscarriage, and it was the one and only time I had sex with someone other than Jacob during our twenty-three-year marriage. I went to New Orleans to promote my first solo novel, *Punishment with Kisses*, at an LGBTQ fiction conference we both love called Saints and Sinners. Jacob and I hadn't talked a lot about our so-called out-of-town rules, even when he went through his transition. He did tell me I had his permission to be with another woman if I really missed lesbian sex. In the beginning, we agreed on non-monogamy with total honesty and disclosure, but that deal morphed over the years as we saw how things happened in real life. Over the years we'd kind of agreed on a Don't Ask, Don't Tell policy sexually akin to "what happens in Vegas, stays in Vegas." But, at least up until that trip to New Orleans, we'd both remained actively monogamous throughout our relationship.

I'd secretly hoped we always would, even if the motivation, as we get older, becomes more about sheer laziness than whether we only have eyes for each other. After all, cheating or maintaining an outside relationship, or even taking the time to get to know another person's body—it all sounds so exhausting, who'd have time for it? Neither of us has time for that kind of extra work. And Jacob is still more attractive than most of the people, male or female, that I meet.

At this point in our relationship Jacob still packed dental dams and condoms and lube into my luggage with little notes like my favorite, for my trip to Las Vegas, that read, "What happens in Vegas stays in Vegas...but you be safe and come home soon."

Each time I saw one of these notes, I'd smile and love him even more.

I'd often brag to my friends and colleagues about how cool and confident he was. When I told my friends about his notes, they thought he must be the most fabulous partner ever.

I don't disagree.

Even if I never took him up on the offer, I've always appreciated it. And now that I'd matured I'd finally started to trust him not to leave me over a one-night stand. I still hope he never has sex with someone else, but I'm finally at a place where I trust he'll come home if he does, not fall in love and blindside me with a huge life change after two decades of marriage.

When I decided to try, one last time to get pregnant, I didn't think all this through. I just decided to be purely selfish, completely irresponsible, and possibly loathsome.

Anyone who's felt the incredibly awful pull of her biological clock ticking—that infernal, mythical, internal countdown of your fertility that I'd spent twenty-five years calling "bullshit"— might understand why I did it. Wanting to get pregnant has been a mysterious and almost hysterical quest. The desire for pregnancy and my inability to conceive have caused me endless guilt and shame. What kind of feminist spends hours thinking about the status of her womb?

I was ashamed to even admit the number of hours I'd spent doing just that (from a failed adoption to the endless navel gazing

Jacob and I used to do as "should we or shouldn't we" potential parents). It felt like a betrayal of all I'd worked for and of the feminist parity I believed in.

Until a decade ago I wasn't really sure I even wanted kids. I just wanted more success. But at some point my desire to have kids catapulted from feeling like I could "take 'em or leave 'em" to an all-consuming desire that seemed to haunt every minute of every day.

I've always been driven and focused on career success. In fact I've been so single-handedly focused on career that I didn't develop my first hobby until I was forty. It's just like me that the one I chose—burlesque dancing—wasn't a typical hobby for a forty-year-old but revolved around my sexuality. I'm so driven that one of my colleagues asked me a few years back, do you want kids because you want to raise kids or just because that'll be another success for you?

I would have been offended if it weren't such a valid question. I wasn't sure I knew the answer, but I was sure I *should*. Why did I want kids? I couldn't say. I couldn't enunciate my reasoning. Maybe because it wasn't rational at all. Maybe it was simply a primal desire.

Once, after Jacob and I'd visited my nieces and nephew, I thought maybe I would be satisfied to devote my energy and maternal impulses to them. If we took them trick-or-treating on Halloween, saved money for their college funds, helped them learn to ride bikes, if we saw them regularly, maybe it could be enough. But we didn't see them enough. We lived in Portland at the time and they lived in Southern California. And they weren't my kids; I'd never have the relationship with them I'd have with my kids of my own.

Would anything but kids of my own really quell this desire?

So when I was forty and stuck in a hotel room in New Orleans watching an earthquake in China kill a hundred thousand people and a cyclone in Myanmar destroying thousands and Ethiopia issued a report about how millions of kids there have only thirty days left of food before they'd starve to death, I admit I was thinking of doing the most ridiculous and selfish thing I could imagine by being convinced I needed to procreate. I kept thinking that we'd spent so much on sperm banks already and whether we would decide to do IVF or adoption or surrogacy in the future, the next step would surely be confusing, expensive, and invasive.

Jacob was three time zones away and it was too early to wake him. I was in New Orleans where everyone else was drinking and dancing and playing, and I wondered, "Why can't I just party, and have fun, and blow off steam, and forget about whether we're qualified to parent foster teens (our latest plan, in case I forgot to mention it) or if I'll ever reproduce or if Jacob and I will have one of those marriages where people say later, 'They were too much in love to share each other with children.'" I liked that idea, but I wasn't sure anyone, especially Jacob, would really buy it.

So I thought, "I should just do it." Right there, right then, do what we'd often joked about: pick up a strange man at a bar and get knocked up. But by that point I was already a crotchety old broad and hadn't been intimate with anyone other than Jacob in eighteen years.

As I explained earlier, I've bragged about my out-of-town rules to anyone who would listen (I consider monogamy uncool), but in in truth, I've never found anyone I was more attracted to than Jacob, nobody I could ever imagine swapping spit or fluids with the way I can with him. Never, not once. I get embarrassed admitting it, it's so…old fashioned, but it's true. Which is a miracle, because of all the relationships I had before him, I was faithful to none. Nada, not one, not even my ex-wife and my high-school boyfriend, both of whom I loved, will always love, like no other. Even at my twentieth high school reunion, a date I had told Jacob about when we first got together as an occasion I would sleep with someone and sow my wild oats, even there I didn't hook up with anyone. (And yes, I got offers, and yes, a woman kissed me, but still no.)

I used to get hit on a lot, constantly. The attention was lovely, and a few times I'd pondered having sex with someone else, rolling the idea around in my head like a pornographic film screening in front of me. And still, I'd never acted, not even that year Jacob couldn't have sex after the accident or another when I was sure Jacob was having an affair of his own with a fellow park ranger.

Now, in New Orleans, forty years old, I argued and reassured myself internally, convincing myself that if I did get pregnant that would be its own reward, a sign our family would grow intact, and if I didn't, I promised myself I'd give up trying to reproduce and accept where we were, maybe consider foster parenting or just growing our brood of Chihuahuas through doggie rescue. I couldn't go through the adoption process again; it was too emotionally grueling.

I wouldn't tell Jacob about the infidelity if I didn't get pregnant; I wouldn't need to. (With our Don't Ask, Don't Tell policy, that seemed right.) I'd just be complete and resolute and sure of what was meant to be. So I did something that will disgust even my single cyber-dating friends. I turned to Craigslist's Personal Encounters section, which I scoured looking for potential one-nighters and, finding none that weren't creepy or desperate or illiterate (yes, a typo in a personal ad makes me *not* want to fuck you), I decided to place my own ad on the website while I was in New Orleans, the city so far from home, the one place on earth I've always thought of as a place of possibilities and where I'm in a safe, security-camera-equipped hotel.

New Orleans is where I fertilized all my dreams (became a journalist, started a magazine, published a novel!), even though I never had a chance to live a single one of them out there. I started college there but didn't finish it there, came out there but only to two people, and got my first major magazine job offer there. It required I leave. So the city and I have some sort of give and take, and it manifests in me always using it up and having to leave, sad and unsatisfied but ever hopeful. I don't know why I didn't think it through better, my sad-sack history of never really getting what I want in New Orleans, but I didn't.

No one sounded remotely palatable. I'm not used to *not* being in control either. When I placed my own ad, I was discreet about my needs and my identity, and as honest as possible about most elements of who I am. The headline read: "Married BBW Lesbian Seeks Cock, in Town 2 Days, 39."

A male friend told me years ago that the fastest way to make a man lose an erection is to say, "I want you to get me pregnant," so I knew not to say that. Moreover, I wanted to pretend that this was a child Jacob and I had made together—this quickie a mere vessel, a sort of meaty sperm-delivery system—and so I didn't want to share anything about my real mission. But staying as close to the truth as possible seemed easy and simple. The final ad looked like this:

I'm a married lesbian who hasn't been with a biological man in over a decade. I'm in town and want to have sex with a man while I'm here. I don't want a relationship. I don't want to know you. I don't want you to sleep over. Let's meet, have a drink, and go back to my hotel, NSA. I'm a sexy BBW, definitely fat and more Anna Nicole curvy than Beyonce curvy. Don't care if you're married or have girlfriend or boyfriend, since I don't want anything beyond this one experience. Discretion is paramount since I'm on a business visit. Don't bring your friends or your wife (okay, that one's negotiable, but honestly I just want a one-time experience with me flat on my back). No hang-ups, no homophobes, don't bother coming to try to convince me your cock will save me from my lesbianism. I'm happy with my life and relationship. Send me a picture and a note.

The minute I put the ad up I worried someone would read between the lines and know who I was, that Jacob would read it and be hurt, that I wouldn't go through with it, or that I would.

I got my first reply via someone's PDA cell phone within thirty seconds from a guy who was really eager to get together. I thought it was a fluke—what kind of crazy guy gets instant alerts from the personal-encounters section of Craigslist on his fucking Blackberry? But then I got flooded with replies, forty-two of them within twenty minutes. The responses kept coming so fast (no pun intended) I had to actually post another ad that said, "Thanks, guys, found my man, no more e-mail." Replies still kept coming for a while until I deleted the whole ad itself. This all happened within an hour. Over eighty guys and two couples wanted to supply the cock I needed.

I asked everyone for photos, and that was intriguing in and of itself: some guys sent a picture with them and their girlfriend or wife or friends, and I wondered about those other people who were now being vaulted through cyberspace as sort of validation of each man's worth (I'm a good man, I swear, the pictures seem to say. Look, I have a beautiful girlfriend).

One man sent me a picture of him with a bride, saying it was a friend's wedding, but I wasn't so sure; he sure looked like the groom. Another one said he couldn't meet up the next day because he had a wedding to attend, and I cringed as I wondered if it might be his own nuptials.

I wondered then if all men are obsessed with the things these men seemed to be obsessed with: sex, fat chicks, lesbians, their own cocks. Many told me long fantasies about how they'd always wanted to have sex with a larger woman, or an older woman, which I apparently must have been since all the guys replying were in their twenties. They dreamed of sexy, curvy cougars and thought I'd fit the bill.

The lesbianism meant another layer of competition; they wanted to use my body to compete with the whole lesbian nation, many offering proof that they could sex me up as good as any woman (many men mentioned that their oral skills were as good as women's, which I generally doubted, unless, like Jacob, they started out as a woman) and had slept with dozens of women. It's a deep insecurity that seems to be deeply ingrained—the belief that women understand other women's bodies better and that few men can really compete with that insider knowledge. I didn't want to be a test subject, my body a marathon site. I wanted a simple ovulation quickie. I realized that wasn't very sexy so I let them think what they wanted. I knew that it was true though; many men aren't as good at oral sex as other women.

It's different if the man once was a woman—or was in a woman's body, that is, and had sex with women. The latter is an explanation, I think, as to why straight women are so attracted to trans men; there's a best-of-both-worlds feel there. If a man has inhabited a body like yours, presumably he'll know how to please it, though I guess that's a stereotype too.

I realized early on that what I was planning wasn't just stupid; it was unsafe and irresponsible as well. I figured that if I met the guy I chose at a public club near my hotel (in this case, at the nightclub at Harrah's casino, aptly named "Masquerade") and then walked past all the security cameras to my room, I'd be safe.

But I didn't kid myself. I knew what a horribly irresponsible thing this was to do. I cried in the bathtub ahead of time because I couldn't stop imagining what Jacob's life would be like if I was killed or even contracted HIV. But I was committed to doing it; that was how insane my stupid baby quest had made me, so to cheer myself up I looked at some porn on the Internet, drank a couple of cocktails, and marched over to the club. He knew what I was wearing and I knew he had on a button-down shirt with a cap. I'd seen a photo of him, but it wasn't that great so I didn't think I'd recognize him. And I didn't.

I should back up. You might wonder how I picked someone from those initial forty-two men? I made a decision that though I was attracted to a much wider range of races and cultures, I'd only sleep with someone who looked similar to Jacob (those blue-eyed blondes I'm attracted to) or someone who looked like me (which I'm generally not that into but wouldn't open me up to endless questions of why my baby looked so different from the two of us). I realized with disgust that I was suddenly planning something very stealthy: not the fucking, but the idea of pretending a baby was a biological product of my husband and me. A closeted baby. I thought about what we'd tell him about his donor, but I left it open in my mind, cart before the horse and all. Eventually the baby would need to know about his donor dad. But what did I even know?

Shaun (not his real name) was twenty-two, young enough to be my son, I think. A mop-topped, dark-haired kid. I wasn't attracted to his photo but decided that since he was twenty-two, his sperm was the most motile, and that since he was a recent grad from my alma matter and lived in my old neighborhood and his e-mail address had the word Atari in it, that had to be a sign he was safe. I thought he was probably a retro hipster who still loved Pong, and that little things like the fact that he attended Tulane were enough to make the union successful. As it turned out, there's a pop punk band called The Ataris. I discovered this days later and felt very old.

Mostly I was glad he had those few similarities, had motile sperm, *didn't* send me a picture of his dick (does any woman respond to that?), and included this line: "I understand and respect that you are not trying to make it a regular thing."

I made a nightcap date with Shaun on Saturday and another with a very good-looking blond named Todd on Sunday (which was ironically Mother's Day, something I was convinced was a sign that I'd conceive). I made a second date because I'd read that scientific studies had proved that sperm literally competes to penetrate, so sex with two men is better than sex with the same man twice, when it comes to conception.

Both men begged to meet with me earlier, as though I were a fleeting fantasy they needed to pin down.

When Shaun found me at the Masquerade I'd already had three drinks and was still nervous. It was loud and I couldn't hear when he said hello, but he tapped my shoulder and was one of the very many guys there wearing caps and button-downs. Though he looked younger than in his photos I assumed it was him. I hoped he wasn't really a high-school student taking AP classes at Tulane. Suddenly I was worried that he was a kid and I'd end up on Dateline's *To Catch a Predator* and not only humiliate myself but also ruin my career.

And it was awkward. Should we shake hands? Embrace? I didn't know. So I said so.

"What's the protocol here?" I asked.

"I don't know," Shaun sheepishly replied.

Great, he was new to this as well. He seemed as nervous as I was, so I dragged him to the ice-covered bar to get a drink, in part to get him loosened up and in part to make sure he was of legal drinking age. I didn't need some Hartford, Connecticut family coming after me for molesting their son.

I was wondering about the whole thing when I noticed as he was signing his credit-card slip he hunched over and used his arm to shield it from me. He's afraid I'm going to roll him, I thought, and I suddenly felt safer and almost motherly.

It'd be okay. I wasn't aroused, but at least I wasn't terrified any longer. He most likely wasn't a serial killer.

So we made chitchat as we searched for a quieter place to talk. I didn't want to know him, I didn't want him to know who I was, but it's hard to make small talk without finding out stuff.

He'd finished Tulane two weeks prior, studied philosophy and something else with international in the title. His girlfriend was a young college girl, nothing serious. He'd always heard about the mystique of having sex with a larger woman and was intrigued. He swore this was his first time answering a Craigslist ad, and I felt quite certain that was true by the naiveté of what he said (like I said, I do get hit on a lot, and I know real players say much more competitive things, in a charmingly persuasive but ultimately unwelcome way).

He was nervous—fidgeting and had a hard time with full-on eye contact. I wasn't sure he was attracted to me either, though he did tell me that I'm attractive and said he was attracted to curvy girls ("And you've got a lot of curves," he admitted), and he told me he'd only slept with "more conventionally attractive girls" at school, which is exactly what every woman wants to hear. Read: skinny. And young. And probably blond.

I admitted I was nervous too. He was surprised. How many women would be so straightforward in an ad, he asked. The men who replied to me did seem to like that I put cock in the title, that I spelled out my limitations, that I didn't want to swallow them up in a relationship.

I was apparently the ultimate fantasy. Many of the guys had confessed they'd always wanted to be with a fat girl; some argued that all men prefer fat girls, but society pins them in and restricts them. My friends used to tell this joke: What do a moped and a fat girl have in common? Answer: They're both fun to ride, but you don't want your friends to see you doing it.

I find the joke funny and offensive alternately, but as more men talk about the beauty standards of women, they sound like they feel cornered, victimized by the same standards as well. Being closeted about your desires is bad, regardless of who you are. I couldn't imagine having to hide my desires.

Shaun was less political about his desires, though we did talk about the environment and the locavore movement and him going home to New York in two weeks and this being his big last hurrah in New Orleans.

For him, I was a hurrah. For me, he was an act of desperation.

I was still anxious, but I couldn't bear to talk any more so we went to my room, Shaun trailing behind me, and then I ran into colleagues and pretended I didn't even know him. I remembered how horrible that had felt when dates would do that with me as a teen, yet I was doing it to someone else. But I didn't want anything getting back to anyone. Still, we reconnected in the elevator and ended up at my room, which had a great view, and since I still didn't feel any "attraction," I had us sit on the couch and asked him to tell me what he liked sexually. I hoped it would turn me on. His turn-ons were as pedantic as everyone's: boobs, flesh, desire.

It wasn't alarming that I felt no attraction. As I said earlier, among the many reasons I'd been "faithful" to Jacob for two decades was that I found no point in having sex with someone I didn't find as attractive as he is (both as Jacob and earlier as Suzy).

I'd found my spouse irresistible for twenty-three years, and if I had one complaint it was that we didn't have enough sex for my liking.

Unlike men who can cheat on the Angelina Jolies of the world, I feel like my sex partners must be as attractive as my spouse or there's no point. You cheat up, not down. And when sex is really good and you're secure in your relationship, there's no point in going outside it. In a good marriage, your partner knows your body so well, he or she can elicit desire and passion and orgasm like no one else. So, like I've already said, I get hit on a lot—at least once a week, often once a day in my thirties, much less now that I'm forty-five—but I don't feel that surge from that type of attention that I still have with Jacob (and admittedly would have with Heather Locklear and Brad Pitt, though I have a lot less access to them than I do to my husband.)

But when you want a baby, you *make* attraction. I wasn't sure Shaun felt any either. He was quiet and reserved and maybe not feeling me. He told me that he loved eating pussy, which was funny because in the last twenty years that was the one thing I'd gotten an awful lot of and it was good, exactly the way I like it. Practice makes perfect, and at that point I wouldn't accept cunnilingus from anyone but Jacob. Plus, no oral was sort of the shield I'd decided on; like hookers who don't kiss, I'd be the queer girl who didn't take accept oral from strangers.

All I cared about was making a baby, so I started teasing his chest and remembered that men don't care about their nipples the way women do, and I thought about how odd men's bodies are—so little on them that's sensitive—and I was glad that trans men like Jacob often keep sensation in their nipples depending on which surgery they choose. They don't want them to be treated like they were boobs anymore, but sensitivity is still cool, especially when you're in your forties and your whole seduction routine includes caressing the neck, slowly working your way down to her nipples. Er, his nipples.

I was rusty. Shaun wasn't even born the last time I slept with a cisgender boy. I didn't kiss him. I wasn't sure if he cared, if it made him feel like a gigolo or not, but kissing is so intimate, I couldn't make myself do it so I didn't. I'd suck his cock, but I wouldn't kiss him.

You can't "see" HIV or most STDs, but it's still pleasing to know somebody's clean and fresh and all, so he thought I was sucking his cock for my own enjoyment. But I was really doing a safety check on him and assuring myself by not using a condom with this dude I won't be signing my death sentence. That's ridiculous, I know. I have a job that involves informing people about how you can tell someone is positive (with a blood test, not a visual inspection), how you can and can't get HIV, and that even if you do, it's now more manageable chronic condition than death sentence (at least in the U.S.). Still I would never want to get HIV and pass it along to Jacob. But delusion is part of the baby-making game, trust me. Was it horrible? No. I'm good at sucking cock— lots of dykes are; most of us are just used to the rubber versions.

When I was ready I said something lame that you'd expect from a Linda Fiorentino movie like, "Let's see what you can do with that bad boy" and pulled him on top of me. Finally, it was going to happen.

Then it did happen: he asked if we should use a condom. Argh. If I said no, I'd be a total skank and he'd freak out and leave. If I said yes, it would sort of moot the point.

I said I didn't care, then, "Wait, should I care?" thinking that would make him feel good about not using one, but the whole conversation was such a mood killer I wondered if that's why men usually hate them, why relying on condom use to stop the spread of HIV has been a failure. At that moment I hated them and wondered if I should bag the whole thing. No sperm equaled a total waste of my time. I didn't know what to do at this point but get this over.

He put on a condom. I was crushed. It literally took less than three minutes. When we were done moments later, he jumped off the bed, dropped the condom in a waste can, and dressed quickly.

We did the "thanks for having me" speech, shook hands, and he was off. The next morning he e-mailed to ask me how he was, you know, what it felt like having a cock inside me so many years without.

I didn't feel compelled to explain that trans men have cocks too. I told him it was lovely. And it was, but probably for different reasons than I could ever explain to him. I was convinced at that moment that I'd be with child soon. You see, as soon as he left I did what may disgust some.

I went to the trash, which was empty save for the soiled condom, and I pulled the rubber out, turned it inside out, and used my whole hand to jam it up inside me and as close to my cervix as possible.

I kept thinking that it was at least five hundred dollars' worth of sperm and I wasn't going to have cheated on my husband without getting what I came for. I spent an hour with my butt in the air, praying to the gods of insemination that these motile little guys would make it to my eggs and that my womb wasn't too dried and dusty for regular use now.

I cried a little bit too, not sure whether I was sad or happy or ashamed or recalcitrant or just emotional. I thought I was all that. I called Jacob and was weepy, but I didn't explain why, in large part because I didn't know why.

I want to come home, I said, I'm tired. Which was also true. Those days, with the long flights every two weeks, waking up in unfamiliar hotel rooms, and the long hours and back-to-back work, and all the travel, I was often very tired and lonely.

Two weeks later I began bleeding and crying. I cried so hard I wanted to stay in bed for days. I obsessed over the waste of sex that I'd had. I was never a puritan, never hung up on monogamy, but now that I'd had sex for reproduction, not pleasure, I couldn't help but focus on what a waste it was to have been "unfaithful" now that I wasn't pregnant.

I'd never before had sex that wasn't about pleasure, *my* pleasure, and I had no idea how to reconcile that experience. I felt unusual for me, ashamed. In an instant I'd become a seed-hungry, closeted soccer mom who cared more about getting knocked up than getting off. I didn't like the change.

I wondered if I should take this to my grave and never tell anyone of my embarrassment and disappointment. I'd promised on that bed that day that I'd give up trying to get pregnant if that day's attempts failed, which I did.

While I was gone Jacob turned in our application to become foster parents. I wasn't sure he was really all that interested in it, but by the time I was home he not only had sent in our application but had enrolled us in a training program and had taken half of the classes needed to be certified.

I was glad. Even though we were then talking about doing something that felt even riskier than pregnancy and infidelity— namely parenting a troubled teenager who didn't "belong" to us—I felt surprisingly up to the task.

And when did I tell Jacob about this whole situation? When I wrote it here in these pages. I had to admit that I did something far more dangerous than have sex with stranger. I had *hope* with a stranger.

JACOB (SUZY)

I've always said that I don't care who Diane has sex with. I've always known that she's more sexual than I am. This was especially true after my back injuries when a side effect of my pain medication was a dip in my already low libido. After the car accident I actually encouraged her to get her needs met elsewhere. With Diane I've always known that I needn't worry about her confusing sex with emotions or falling for a one-night stand.

I also believe implicitly in the fact that a woman's body is hers and hers alone, and she is free to make decisions about what, or who, she does with it.

But I don't want to know about it.

I'm not crazy jealous, but I don't enjoy imagining someone else touching the woman I love. And I think it's hard *not* to visualize those images. So I haven't wanted to know. I admit it was a little difficult to read her description about that experience.

At the beginning of this multi-year journey of writing this memoir Diane and I agreed to be brutally honest, and even acknowledge things that we've never told other people about. Will we live to regret that decision? Perhaps.

In our modern world, unfettered honesty can be a dangerous thing. Diane and I both write about our real lives, and sometimes those pieces receive less than positive responses. Friends and loved ones have occasionally been offended that we've mentioned their names, or remembered an event happening differently than they recall, or they're simply embarrassed to be connected or related to us when we do or say certain things.

These days people's perceptions can almost be more important than the "truth." As public figures we are, whether we like it or not, role models, so there's pressure for us to be a model queer couple. In that sense, we know our private decisions are often scrutinized and judged. If someone in the LGBTQ community thinks we're falling down on our responsibilities in representing our tribe, they don't hesitate to tell us.

I'm sure some trans men would find it particularly offensive that Diane slept with a cisgender guy. It's sometimes hard not to feel inadequate as a man when you're trans, especially when you're comparing yourself to non-trans men. I know that nearly every man in America worries about the size of his penis or his sexual prowess, but most of them didn't start out in a female body. Most of them have homegrown, all-natural dicks that—regardless of size—have some inherent advantages over the man-made versions or their silicon replacements.

Okay, maybe it's just me. Plenty of trans guys have completely embraced their imperfect bodies. Some of them insist silicon is better than flesh because it can be switched out for sizes or shapes that best pleasure one's partner. Others who've never had and never will have bottom surgery find a way to accept their "female" anatomy, arguing that when it's on a man, a vagina isn't inherently female. I envy some of these trans guys. I wish I was a little more at peace with the body I now have.

I pass perfectly well in public and have been propositioned by straight women and gay guys alike, so I'm pretty confident in my maleness being publically validated. But when I get home and take off my clothes—well, that's when my confidence falters.

In *Just Add Hormones*, Matt Kailey talks about standing naked in front of a mirror, telling himself, "This is a trans man's body." I've tried that. Since we don't have a full-length mirror, to see my whole body requires a lot of acrobatics and standing on the bathroom sink, but I have confronted my physical reflection.

It's true that, since transitioning, I no longer see a woman's body reflected back at me. And I'm far less disconnected from the body in the mirror. I know that's my body, and I'm thrilled that it doesn't look like a woman's body. But I'm a perfectionist, and I can't seem to get past some of the ways my body differs from that of a cisgender dude's. It will never be what it would have been if I'd been born a boy. Surgery can only do so much.

But back to Vegas—how do I feel now that I know? Am I as open-minded and easy-going about extramarital sexual encounters now that they're no longer theoretical? Actually, I've always assumed that Diane had utilized her out-of-town freedoms and I've been fine with it. But it is true that actually knowing and reading details about a specific encounter is more difficult.

If Diane had said she'd chosen to sleep with some bio guy because she hadn't "been with a man" for twenty years, I would've been crushed. It's important to me that Diane sees me as a "real man," even though I know cisgender guys have some qualities I'll never have (of course not all of those are positives).

But I'm not surprised that Diane acted on a scenario we'd joked about—picking some random guy to have sex with just for his seed. After all, not being able to conceive via sex has always seemed one of the cruelest realities in gay and lesbian couples.

And for some people it works. All you need is one night or one syringe or one foster application. It's never been that simple for us. Still, I think I would've been thrilled if Diane had returned with a Vegas baby, even though that hardly seems like the best way to choose a baby daddy.

But it is a little like the episode of *The Simpsons* where Homer tries to help Apu and Manjula get pregnant by re-creating some common sites of (teen) conception. Going to Vegas is a little like driving up to Makeout Point dressed as teenagers getting it on before the boy goes off to war or college (there were script problems, Homer says in the episode).

Actually, I think Diane's Vegas story is kind of cute. She talks about missing me, she admits she hasn't wanted to turn in her out-of-town chip or take advantage of the condoms I add to her luggage. In twenty-three years her greatest "infidelity" was another attempt to grow our family, like the times she's brought home a stray dog that needs a home.

And I wouldn't call it infidelity; Diane has never been unfaithful a day in our relationship. Her faith in me and commitment to me haven't wavered in all our time together. And that's saying a lot considering when we met Diane didn't even believe people could be monogamous because she'd never known a couple that was.

While knowing my parents may have given her some insight into the potential of a long-term relationship, I bet Diane has been influenced more by our friends Homer and Marge Simpson and the way they keep their love strong despite the many difficulties they've faced over the preceding decades.

The Simpsons aren't just role models. The show has become an important touchstone in our relationship.

Over the years, Diane and I have become super fans. We watch it daily. We record every episode, whether new or syndicated or repeated for the fiftieth time. We own every season ever released on DVD. We fall asleep to *The Simpsons* every night. We collect *Simpsons* action figures and display play sets, like the one featuring Homer in a male muumuu, which he dons in one episode after intentionally gaining sixty pounds to get on disability and avoid doing five minutes of mandatory calisthenics at work.

Diane and I have watched every episode of *The Simpsons* that has ever aired and have seen many of them so many times we've memorized the dialogue. *The Simpsons* are such a part of our private culture that we often quote the show in our private conversations and embarrass ourselves by doing so around other people who often have no freaking idea what we're talking about.

But the slightest reference to a particular scene—say one of us snarling the word "Diddily!" to the other—will lead us to conjure up the episode (like when Marge runs over werewolf Flanders) and laugh out loud.

For us, *The Simpsons* is a reminder of numerous shared experiences, and every time we reference a previous episode, it reminds us of our bond, of our shared experiences, our shared values, our shared sense of humor.

We shorthand other cultural references, of course. In the movie *Dave*, for example, Kevin Kline's character thanks his long-suffering wife, played by Sigourney Weaver, for doing a public appearance (they play the president and first lady) with the phrase, "Thanks for doing this, Ellen." For decades, we've used that as shorthand as well, to thank the other person for doing some unpleasant task neither of us wants to do. We say it at least once a week.

But *The Simpsons* really feeds us the most. I can't say it saved our marriage, but I can say it gave us the shared language with which to help make it thrive. People always ask, "What keeps you two together through thick and thin?"

The Simpsons. Chips and salsa. Whenever we had important decisions to make or major problem to work out, we'd take a break and go eat chips and salsa. When we were younger it was a great option, because certain bars offered free, all-you-can eat chips and salsa for the price of a blended margarita. Sitting down to mull over life with chips and salsa has remained a favored pastime.

And the understanding that no one else is as *Simpsons*-literate or *Simpsons*-tolerant as we are helps keep us together. Who else would get it when I respond to their bad day by texting, "It sounds like you just need some reassurance"? Who else would provide the perfect response: "LOL. Zzzzz."?

The Simpsons was a gateway drug.

I may have grown up without TV, but watching *The Simpsons* with Diane broke down years of resistance, and soon I was addicted. It led to *Futurama*, *American Dad*, *Family Guy*, and even more eclectic titles like *Dr. Katz*, *Home Movies*, and *The Oblongs*. Eventually they broke my resistance altogether and I moved on to harder stuff: *Law & Order* and *CSI*.

Diane and I have watched it all together. In doing so, we've broadened our shared experiences and solidified our shared values.

Back on the farm, I would never have thought that television would become such an important part of my life, let alone that TV would save my marriage. But in some ways, it has.

If it weren't for *The Simpsons*, we wouldn't even call each other queerly beloved.

CHAPTER FOURTEEN

PROCTOR PARENTING

JACOB (SUZY)

Diane and I became foster parents in the fall of 2008. We'd considered it many times before, but then seemed like a perfect opportunity because we were living in a five-bedroom house and our housemate/friend Athena had moved to New York, leaving us with a half-empty house. We'd long thought about being foster parents, and this seemed the perfect solution to our many needs.

We went to a foster-parenting orientation without realizing that it was run by an organization that subcontracted with the Oregon Department of Human Services, rather than being DHS itself. Choosing from several programs, we decided on one that worked with adjudicated youth; in particular it focused on therapeutic proctor parenting of teenage boys who'd been through the juvenile justice system primarily because they'd committed a crime of a sexual nature.

Later, when I realized we weren't working with DHS directly, I contacted their office just to see if they were doing any specific outreach or recruiting of LGBTQ parents, considering the high number of queer and trans runway youths who congregated on the streets of Portland. They didn't. At the time, they made no effort to place LGBTQ youth with LGBTQ foster parents.

Sigh.

Before we became foster parents we had to go through a background check and get fingerprinted, which was all old hat for us because when I got my first big ranger job I'd been through an intensive background check in which a private investigator spoke to our neighbors, family members, and coworkers. I had to provide a list of every person I'd ever shared a house with, going back to high school. I had to go through a lie-detector test. I had to have a psychological exam. I had to write down any time that I'd ever broken a law, no matter how small or big or whether or not I'd been caught (even smoking dope in college). So the background check for the proctor program didn't seem that significant.

We also had to complete forty hours of training before we were certified for our specific foster-care program, and then from that point on we had to have a minimum of twenty-four hours of training each year. Our house was evaluated by the Department of Human Services, which conducted quarterly home visits to certify that the home continued to meet the demands of foster parenting.

We were accepted into the program with the adjudicated teens, working with a child- and family-services organization that had been around since 1984. At one time this program was actually run out of a residential facility, like a therapeutic boarding school or prison-light, depending on who you asked, but many states began closing these types of residential units after evidence demonstrated that children did better in individual homes than in group settings. Now the organization placed clients in therapeutic homes staffed by trained proctor parents, who helped support the educational and therapeutic goals of the program.

Some of the rules included that the kids had to be within sight or hearing distance whenever they weren't in school, in the bathroom, or in their bed for the night. Since we were in a two-story house, we had to install security cameras in the basement that we could monitor from upstairs, and we put cameras and door alarms in the upstairs hallways and bedroom doors.

Each boy had his own bedroom and wasn't allowed to spend time in the bedroom of anyone else. But we had a large living room and a huge room in the basement with an enormous projection-style big-screen TV. We put in a couple of used couches and hooked up an Xbox to the TV. We also had an eight-in-one game table on which they could play pool or air hockey or poker. And we set up tons of other games in the basement family room.

The boys were only allowed a certain amount of video-game playing and TV watching each week, and we had to monitor both activities heavily. Some kids would probably never have left the basement, but, as I quickly discovered, our boys didn't like to be alone. They craved attention.

When I originally became a proctor parent I thought I would be able to continue doing the work I was doing at home. At the time I'd recently stopped writing my TransNation column and instead was doing freelance writing for publications like *Just Out* in Portland, *Windy City Times* in Chicago, SheWired.com, and both *Curve* and *Bitch* magazines.

I was also working at KBOO, a local public-access radio station where I contributed to news stories and helped with the LGBTQ show, *Out Loud*, before I launched and co-hosted a show on gender. *Gender Blender* was an hour-long talk show that aired once a month.

Earlier that year, Diane and I had also started a public queer monthly literary series called QLiterati. We recruited authors, set up the space, cooked snacks, put together raffles and door prizes, and managed all the PR (designing, printing, and posting flyers; writing and distributing press releases).

Although none of these projects were full time and most of them didn't pay, they required us to put in a fair amount of work each month. But I couldn't see how proctor parenting would really interfere in these other things. I was naïve. I spent most of my time at home lying on the floor with my laptop balanced on my knees. How could having the boys interfere with that?

The answer: by needing constant attention.

Proctor parenting was a little like visiting Diane's nephew and nieces. From the moment we walk into their house until we leave hours later, the kids follow me around, tugging on my arm and screaming, "Uncle, Uncle, Uncle." They want me to pick them up, watch them do dangerous stunts, play games with them. They want my undivided attention.

And that's how the boys were too. They would constantly call "Diane, Jacob," to make sure we were listening or watching or just there. I found it really difficult to work in the same room as them because they were constantly interrupting me. It wasn't enough just to be in the same room with them. They needed me to talk to them, engage with them. They needed my active attention.

Even working while the boys were away at school turned out to be difficult. They went to a private school that was part of their therapeutic program. They weren't allowed to travel on public transportation themselves, so every morning I drove them to the campus. Then usually I had to meet with someone from the program to talk about the progress and problems facing the group as a whole or our boys specifically. I would have to pick up the mail, read updates or policy changes, or attend new trainings for foster parents.

I'd get back home by ten a.m. or so. Sometimes I'd stop at the grocery store or do other errands on the way home, because taking the boys into public spaces could be stressful because of the program rules and their psychological needs, and if the boys had lost privileges that week they weren't allowed to accompany us to stores anyway.

The boys had chore assignments and usually helped cook dinner, but we still needed to engage in various activities to help the household routine run smoothly. We had to maintain chore charts, go over their homework, write daily progress reports, and keep track of medication and allowances. Sometimes we had to search the boys' rooms while they were gone, checking for various contraband items.

I couldn't do some personal-maintenance chores when the boys were at home because they required me being in another room. So, while they were away, I cleaned our bedroom, bathed, did our laundry, and returned phone calls.

I'd barely have gotten to my real work when it would be time to leave and go pick the boys up from school. Often I'd also have to arrive early in order to speak with one of the teachers or therapists because we worked closely with them to meet the boys' educational, behavioral, and therapeutic goals.

Proctor parenting was a full-time job, and I pretty much stopped freelancing to focus on the demands of the kids and the requirements of the program they were in.

Because of the nature of the program we had to lock a lot of our reading and viewing material away. I don't mean we had shelves of pornos or X-rated movies and books. But we'd been childless adults for nearly two decades, and most of the books and movies on our shelves were aimed at adults. The program had a list of approved movies, and we put away anything that wasn't on that list—actually we put away all the films. We just put some of them in deep storage and others within reach, because anything rated higher than a G was suspect. We could show them PG movies at our discretion and if they weren't having any behavioral problems that week.

One of the program's principles was that exposure to unfiltered media was dangerous for children. They wanted to control the messages and content that the kids in the program were consuming. They did this by outlawing all forms of media—magazines, books, movies, music, comic books, video games—and then slowly adding some screened items back in.

They not only wanted to avoid sexual situations but also inappropriate language, violence, and depictions of male-female relations that weren't based on an equal footing. (Although many of the clients identified as gay, bisexual, or questioning, the program seemed particularly aimed at eliminating hetero imagery, perhaps because victimology was rooted in part in misogyny.)

So we had to buy lockable glass doors for our bookshelves. At the time we had four floor-to-ceiling shelving units covered with glass doors and then locked with chains and padlocks.

We also had to lock up all our medication and move anything that might be considered dangerous from the bathroom—anything sharp, any kind of medication or cleaning products that could be swallowed that would prove harmful, as well as unexpected items like plungers and tampons. Yes, we had to keep tampons under lock and key because the boys could either sexualize or do self-injurious things with them.

We told the program that we could handle one or maybe two boys. We outfitted two rooms through IKEA and Craigslist. They placed two boys with us. One week each month parents were required to take a respite, which meant they wouldn't have kids in their home for two days and they could have couple time, leave the state without special permission, watch adult TV shows or R-rated movies, or just veg and recover. It was a great system. But it meant that on the other three weekends someone else's kids might be placed at our home. So while we had two boys during the week, on weekends it wasn't uncommon for us to have four.

This was during the time when Diane was still flying to San Francisco from our home in Portland every three weeks, and she'd be gone for a week to ten days each time. Sometimes she'd be out of town when I'd have four teenage boys at home. To say it was overwhelming is an understatement. I remember crying on the phone, telling her that I hadn't gotten into this to be a single father.

The second boy that was placed with us was assigned to us in part because the program was aware he was struggling with gender issues. But we weren't allowed to tell him who we were, or least who I was.

That's not quite fair: we could be open about some things. If we'd been still been a lesbian couple, we wouldn't have had to hide that fact from the boys. There were other gay parents in the program. In fact that was one of the main reasons we had been drawn to this specific program in the first place. When we went to an orientation meeting and talked to the other parents, we felt like we'd found a place where we belonged. The group included two gay couples, an African-American lesbian couple, and an old but unmarried straight hippie couple. We felt that we fit in perfectly.

But I wasn't allowed to be out about my gender identity. This was the case even though the program seemed trans friendly and one of the teachers was a trans woman.

I have to admit that there was something nice about not being out. It was really the first time since I transitioned when I wasn't. And there was something nice about having these boys respond to me like I was just one of the guys. Not knowing my history meant they didn't see me differently from the other proctor fathers. And there was something really wonderful about that.

But I don't think closets are healthy.

Anytime someone tells you that you can't be open about who you are, you suffer psychological damage. And when you have to be in a closet in your own home? It's oppressive. Behind the closed doors of your home is the one place you're supposed to be able to be free to be yourself. But I was supposed to keep the boys in the dark about that part of me.

This was true even after Diane was allowed to tell one particular boy that she edited a lesbian publication. This was also true even after this same kid received special permission to accompany us to QLiterati! and give his own open-mic readings.

The program was basically saying it was okay to be openly and proudly gay, but it wasn't okay to be transgender.

One day the program called and asked us to come in early and meet with our proctor son and his therapist. When we got there the boy was hysterical. He was sobbing, trying to explain that he'd violated our privacy but hadn't meant to. He was ashamed, apologetic. He wouldn't look us in the eyes.

Diane and I didn't know what the hell he was talking about.

The gist of it was that he'd been using the computer in class to do some research and had looked up my name. I'm not sure if he was supposed to do that. I think he pretended he'd stumbled on my name researching something for his class, but I believe he'd just Googled me.

As a "professional" trans person, my transgender status has never been a secret. I worked in the media as an openly transgender journalist, so articles include my byline. My online bio at the time started, "Jacob Anderson-Minshall is a trans writer." It was no secret: I was proud to be trans.

But, because the program forced me to be in the closet, the boy thought he wasn't supposed to be aware of my status. Inadvertently my silence about my gender had given him the sense that it was something I was ashamed of, something I didn't want other people to realize about me. I tried to assure him that I wasn't upset with him, that I wasn't embarrassed about my gender, that it was okay for him to know.

But the program still insisted that he shouldn't tell the other boys, not even the other boy living in our house. Now the program not only demanded my silence but the silence of our foster kid as well. Now they were demanding that he deceive the others in the program, to keep a secret from those in his group therapy and the boy he shared a home with.

I should mention that the program puts an extremely high premium on truthfulness. The boys have to admit to every terrible thing they've ever done or thought about doing or fantasized about doing. When requested by the program, they have to submit to a lie detector, and if they're found to be deceptive, they can be immediately terminated from the program.

Since most of the boys in this program were in the correctional system, being terminated from the program would essentially mean being sent back to juvenile detention or prison, depending on their age. So the boys are told that truthfulness is next to godliness. It's the thin line between them and incarceration.

But now, in an entirely schizophrenic manner, the program was telling this boy that he had to lie—to every other boy in the program.

We objected.

To no avail.

As I said, the program staff and we all knew this boy was struggling with gender questions of his own. After he learned about my gender he was like a sponge for information. He got permission to read books on the subject—in his room where no one else could see the titles. He got permission to tag along when I hosted Gender Blender.

His own wheels started turning in overdrive. One day he stopped struggling. He stopped questioning. He announced to Diane and me that he wasn't a real boy. He said, "I am a girl."

We didn't say, "I know." But we did feel like we had to say something. We had to respond.

It's the kind of announcement that demands action. We asked him what he wanted to do. We asked him if he wanted to wear women's clothing.

He said he didn't want to do that, but he'd like to try on makeup, at home, when none of the other boys were around. Since our other proctor boy at the time had special permission to play football at a local school, Diane agreed they'd have a girls' night while I went to the next game.

We asked him if he wanted to have a female name, if he wanted to change pronouns.

He said no, he didn't need to be called a different name. He thought asking his peers and teachers to use female pronouns would just be confusing and lead to harassment. He said the main thing he wanted was for his peers in the program to know because they were picking on him because of his effeminate behavior. He thought if his peers knew he was trans, that he was really a girl, then they'd understand why he acted more "like a girl" than a boy.

After we'd moved to Portland I met Jenn Burleton, the founder of an organization called TransActive, a nonprofit aimed at supporting transgender children. Jenn had transitioned in the 1960s or '70s, when she was still a teenager. She did this by stealing her mother's birth-control pills. In essence she started herself on hormone treatments.

When our proctor child came out as transgender, I arranged for us to have lunch with Jenn. She also brought along a young trans woman who'd transitioned as a teenager. We ate and chatted, and then Jenn talked about the new Oregon laws that required that schools and public agencies provide accommodations for transgender students to live and dress and be addressed in the pronoun that most suited them.

She said that TransActive would be happy to step in and advocate for our proctor kid, but in order to avoid any antagonism with the school, it would be best to start with the boy telling a staff member he identified as trans and see how they responded. It needed to come from the child first, and then we could step in as advocates to support him and work with the program to create a supportive environment at school.

The next day our proctor kid went to school. By the time I made it home, he'd spoken with his therapist. He'd come out as trans and said he was really a girl, and though he'd decided he wanted to be called Dani at our home, at school he just wanted the other students to understand who he was.

This caused an uproar.

But I wouldn't know that until the end of the day. In the meantime, the program called his "real" parents and talked to a lawyer and contacted the state oversight agency to report us.

We were nearly kicked out of the program. We'd overstepped our bounds and had stepped on his parents' legal rights by allowing him to meet and talk to Jenn without them present. We were reminded that we weren't his parents and were told that his parents had wanted us kicked out of the program. They were considering a lawsuit. We were reminded that the program was for boys, and boys only. The program had once allowed a trans girl in, but they'd required her to go by a masculine name and wear pants while in the program.

I reminded them that new laws had gone into effect that protected transgender students in the state of Oregon.

The minute the boy's bio parents got involved, he recanted. He changed his story and said he wasn't really trans. He claimed that Diane and I had pushed him into making the proclamation. He said he was just confused and we'd taken advantage of that to forward our own agenda. The things he was now saying didn't sound like him. They didn't sound like his words. We were pretty sure they had originated with his parents. We were pretty sure they'd come straight from his overbearing mother's mouth.

But it didn't matter where we thought it had originated. Once he verbalized it, it had ramifications. We had to be investigated. He was immediately moved to another proctor home.

The program didn't really think we'd pressured him. But they did think we'd overstepped our bounds. They felt we were lucky to get off with a warning that the pressure of trying to come out to his parents had been too overwhelming and so he'd backed down and turned the blame on us. We could have told them he wasn't ready to come out to his parents. But we'd naively thought he didn't have to.

Maybe we *had* forgotten our place. Maybe we'd forgotten that we were responsible for our foster kids but had no parental rights.

I would have liked to say it would never happen again, though I'm not sure that would be true.

But we didn't let our guard down around the gender-confused kid again, even when he eventually came back to live with us. We didn't exactly blame him, but we also didn't trust him after that. He'd hurt us, even if he hadn't meant to, even if he was just trying to protect himself.

We were angry, but we were angry at the system, which put us in the uncomfortable position of parenting a child we weren't really allowed to parent. For giving us a gender-confused kid, telling us to help him, and not allowing us to help him talk about how he saw his gender. For making me be in a closet. For making him come out of one.

Just as a side note: after we stopped being proctor parents, we were called and asked if we would come back because they had a girl who really needed a place to stay. Apparently it wasn't as impossible for the program to allow a girl into the all-boys' program as we'd been led to believe. Apparently it was just trans girls they couldn't abide.

❖

Ever since I took women's studies classes in college, I've been aware of how advertising uses women bodies to sell products. But it wasn't until I was charged with protecting these boys from being triggered by sexually evocative stimuli that I really became aware of how much our world is overflowing with sexualized imagery.

We live in a very adult world, but children live in it with us, and they're exposed to a surprising level of adult material. And I don't just mean what they find online.

As proctor parents with the program, we became hyperaware of sexualized imagery.

We carefully monitored the small screen—not just the content of the television shows but of commercials. We'd keep a finger on the remote at all times so we could instantaneously change the channel if a woman appeared scantily dressed. Even driving around town sometimes we'd pass a video store and see a giant picture of the latest *Tomb Raider* video game or the latest movie poster. Basically whatever the ad, it always seemed to feature a woman in a provocative pose, wearing tight or little clothing.

Women and feminists are obviously very aware of how the female form is utilized to draw men's attention and cause them to spend money, but from a personal point of view it was after testosterone altered my brain chemistry that I really began to notice. I focus more on images now; they motivate me more, and they definitely arouse me more. I now see the sexy women selling things and respond differently than I would have in the past.

But as proctor parents we had to become even more aware, hyper alert, to what imagery was around us and how it might impact one of the boys. Because that imagery did trigger our kids into having thoughts that, in the past, had led them to violence, seeing them now could let their desires override their therapy. And because of that fact, we started seeing the world in a very different way. We were sort of shocked by how much sexualized material children are confronted with every day, even when they don't go out of their way to find it.

Of course in order to protect the boys from being triggered, we had to know what kind of things would trigger them. Sometimes it was difficult, emotionally and psychologically, to know about the boys' histories. But the program believed it was important for proctor parents to understand what the boys had done in order to provide a safe place for them to grow and change.

So we had access to their criminal records to understand what charges they had been convicted of or what they'd admitted to doing. We also often had access reports from psychotherapists or social workers who'd evaluated the boys.

Not surprisingly, most of the boys had also been victims themselves. It was different knowing that they had been victimized and actually reading detailed accounts of what they'd been exposed to.

It's traumatic to know this information, to have those images in your head, to know what they and others have been capable of and what they had been through, which was often as bad or worse than their own crimes. There's actually a form of psychological stress known as vicarious trauma that caregivers can suffer in circumstances where they have to know these details. It comes from empathizing and feeling responsible for what these kids had been through, what they had done and had been done to them, but it leaves the caregiver (or the therapist, who is the most common victim of vicarious trauma) with a form of post-traumatic stress disorder, as though the trauma had happened to them.

Diane dealt with this type of stress by avoiding the material. Her mother was molested as a child so Diane knew what abuse did to kids, but she always saw these kids in our care as victims first, perpetrators second. But I felt like it was my duty to know. It was important to know, for example, if one of our proctor kids had ever hurt an animal. I needed to be able and protect my family and to provide personalized care to the kids in our home. But that didn't make it less difficult to read the records and reports. I had to try hard not to look at these kids differently after I'd had full disclosure. They were just kids, yet if you described some of their actions to someone else, they might insist those were the actions of someone evil. A monster.

But they *were* just kids. And yet…some of them were also sexual predators. All of our boys had been victimized. All of them had victimized other people—usually people younger and weaker than themselves.

In the United States, something like one in four women will be the victim of sexual assault in her lifetime. Among my acquaintances, I think that rate is much higher.

And since a disproportionate number of my friends and family have been victimized by others in a sexual manner, it was all the more difficult to know that these boys had victimized others in that way, even if they had first been victimized by someone else.

And yet we were able to set these things aside and just see the boys as troubled kids. We bonded with the kids in our house. And for the most part, we loved being parents. We relished the Sunday-morning breakfasts, singing karaoke or playing air hockey in the basement, teaching them things we had long ago lost interest in but which they found fascinating. Every night when I brought them home from school, Diane would ask, "What did you learn today?" and she'd expect a real, thoughtful answer. When Diane was home, with one of our kids, she'd watch *iCarly* and *Penguins of Madagascar* and play in the yard with the dogs and answer every "why" question he had stored up during his twelve years of parental neglect. She pushed out of her mind the fact that that same kid couldn't stop fantasizing about, say, binding and raping elderly women, because she saw the child he really was and the mother he desperately needed.

But it could be hard. As we'd learned earlier, the kids almost all had birth families they would be going home to. Those families continued to make decisions regarding their care, and we came to see that those families were often the root of their problems. It didn't help that those families were often homophobic and uneducated and dealing with their own mental-health issues.

However, no matter how absentee or problematic or damaging those parents were, at the end of the day they were the parents, and the crimes of their sons hadn't diminished their parental rights. When they completed the program, most of the boys would return to their birth families, as long as they had a family that wanted them (some didn't). And they were allowed to visit those families as well, often working up to full weekend visits with their parents that would leave them despondent or angry or suicidal come Sunday night. We did damage control with the aftermath of those visits.

And we had another problem: the kids kept leaving. Although it could take the boys eighteen months to two years to complete the entire program, we didn't always get boys when they first started it or keep them throughout their tenure. So, every few months, it seemed like another new boy came into our house. Others stayed for longer periods, but that made their leaving even more painful.

Basically, it was just difficult to deal with the loss that occurred each time one of the boys left our home, regardless of whether he was graduating from the program, moving to another house, or being returned to a detention center. For Diane, it was the constant loss that was the greatest.

❖

We also struggled with the program's educational arm. We'd been told that most of the kids in the program were behind their schoolmates. But rather than catch up, the program's educational arm went at a glacial pace. In a time when parents across America were complaining about the huge amount of homework their kids were being required to do, the proctor boys often came home with only one sheet of problems to work through. No books. No reading assignments. Nothing.

During the summer things became much worse. While public schools were on summer vacation, our boys were in a year-round program. Since they were behind educationally, we thought the program would use this time as an opportunity to catch up.

During the summer months, when the boys came home from school and Diane would ask what they'd learned, the boys kept talking about the films they'd seen in class that day. While many of the movies had some educational value—say, the biography of Vince Lombardi—they weren't tied to any coursework or educational goal. They might watch a documentary about slavery during math or an educational program about dinosaurs for English.

The program brushed Diane's complaints aside. "You have to understand," they said. "When we were a residential program the teachers were on a regular schedule and had summers off. When we switched to a proctor home environment, we felt we needed to have year-round programs because many of our parents work outside the home. The teachers resent having to be here at all."

During the summer months, the "school" really became a glorified day-care center. Diane was pushing the boys in our care to plan for college, to shoot for their dreams, but the program would consider these boys a success simply if they didn't commit another crime. If they became high-school dropouts who never sexually assaulted again, they were considered a statistical success.

The program is proud of its success rate, which is one of the highest for any program of its kind. It's truly remarkable and does make a positive impact on these clients' lives. It's good at what it does, but it's also good at management, at making decisions that ultimately impact the bottom line. For example, the program has a very diligent screening process. They have a good sense of what kind of client will be successful versus who might fail, and they don't accept clients they don't think they can help.

This isn't a bad thing. They have limited resources and their space is in high demand. They have more applicants than they can accept, so it's only wise for them to focus on the kids they can most likely help.

Once the client has been accepted, there are other ways to… well, massage things, so their success rates continue to remain high. For example, the program only tracks the clients who successfully complete their program. Again, this seems reasonable.

But it seemed to play a part in the decision process whenever a client was being considered for termination from the program. Basically, if staff members realize they'd accepted someone who they'd come to think wouldn't be successfully rehabilitated, they had an incentive to see that client dropped from the program altogether. We watched this scenario play out as some clients were given multiple chances to get their act together while others were quickly dropped from the program when they began to struggle.

Another element is the definition of "success." For the program, success meant having a client who didn't reoffend. When you come at this from a criminal-justice perspective and view these clients as sexual predators, then preventing them from reoffending for the rest of their lives *is* an unqualified success.

But when you view the clients as the children they are, is it enough that they never sexually assault another person? Is it enough that they stay out of jail? Is that success?

If it were your child, would that be an acceptable measure of success?

Certainly, there's a clear choice between having a highly successful college graduate, businessman, home owner who's also a serial offender versus a couch-surfing high-school dropout, gas-station attendant who never reoffends. But are those really the only options? If this were your kid, wouldn't it matter whether they finished high school, went to college, got a good job, could reach any of their dreams?

Wouldn't having a stressful, low-paying job and seeing your life go nowhere actually threaten your chances of recidivism the way stress has an impact on adult recidivism rates?

❖

Things became particularly rough for us after we took in a very young client, whose name we can't mention because of privacy concerns, so let's just call him Parker. He was twelve when he came to live with us. Maybe he was too young.

The program works on the idea that a teenager's brain is a brain in flux. A teenager's brain hasn't stopped growing. In fact it's going through the greatest growth spurt it ever will, and because of that fact the program believes that intervention during this period of development could make a lifelong impact on the behavior of these kids.

Many studies have suggested that in adult populations, sexual offenders are the most difficult to rehabilitate, the most likely to reoffend. So making a difference when these children are still young can be the difference between a lifetime as a sexual predator and one of a happy, healthy, non-predatory man.

But perhaps Parker's brain hadn't yet developed enough for him to truly grasp what the program needed him to understand. For example, he was clearly struggling with acknowledging that he'd done something wrong and had victimized someone when the injured party had never said he'd injured them. Although a significant age difference existed between him and his victim, he truly felt like they were both just kids, both willing participants. He didn't seem to understand that he was the predator because of that difference.

When they first accepted Parker, the administrators acknowledged to us that he might be too young to succeed. They thought it would be better if he waited another year. But no one liked the idea of this tween spending the next twelve months in the detention facility with other older, hardened kids where he'd been incarcerated.

Parker was also at a disadvantage because of his appearance. Although he was still just a child, he had the body of high-schooler. He was a tall and gangly man-child, and somehow that made others view him as more threatening than they would if he were small. We witnessed this reaction firsthand, in fact.

A little while after he came to the program, another boy the same age was accepted as well. He came to live with us too. Our caseworkers regarded us as a couple that did well with young kids, those who weren't quite teenagers yet. This new child was very different from Parker. He looked like a tiny pixie standing next to a giant when the two of them were together.

This new little kid was charming and cute and hiding sociopathic tendencies behind his innocent façade. We started noticing that he behaved very differently when he was in front of us versus when he was downstairs alone with one of the other boys. He didn't realize our cameras had microphones attached and that we could hear his lies and the way he seemed to manipulate other boys to do something and then tell a staff member on them.

But our reports of his behavior so contrasted with the experience of other staff members that we were dismissed as biased. In the long run he was placed in another house, where it would quickly become evident that he was exactly the problem child we said he was. But even when other proctor parents reported similar behavior, some staff members simply refused to believe that the sweet, innocent boy they saw at school had them bamboozled.

This was what bothered us most—that the staff could support some kids to the ends of the earth, regardless of what evidence came to light of their rule breaking. But other kids committed similar infractions and were literally handcuffed and dragged out of the school by their probation officers that very day. (When the program kicks a child out, it's reported to their probation officer who will come transport them either to a lockdown treatment facility or to juvenile detention, often times in handcuffs.)

I remember one time having a meeting with Parker's therapist, and the therapist was very angry at Parker because he thought the kid had lied to him. As I've explained, honesty was prized in the program.

But there was actually no proof that Parker had lied. Remember that the kids in the program had to write detailed accountings of every offense they had ever done—whether they had been caught for it or not. Well, Parker hadn't mentioned one thing.

I'd read his file. I knew about the behavior in question. It was in Parker's psychiatric evaluation, a rumor that was essentially unverified so there was no way to know if it was true or not. There was no official accusation. No one ever came forward to say they actually witnessed this act. Apparently the stepmother had said something to his father, who called and told the therapist, and the therapist acted like it was new information that Parker had refused to disclose (which I'll never understand since he had access to the same reports I read) and that it was a bona fide fact.

It seems worth mentioning that the father had relinquished his parental responsibilities to Parker by putting him on a plane from somewhere in the South to Oregon and then calling the kid's estranged mother to say, "He's your problem now. I relinquish my parental rights. His plane lands in three hours."

The mother actually lived two hours away from the airport. Our foster son never talked about how this experience felt, but it sounds like it could have been terrifying to be shipped off alone to an airport without any idea who (if anyone) would come get him.

Yet the therapist took this man's accusation at face value and therefore believed Parker had lied to him. I thought the therapist was a professional who wouldn't be personally hurt by a kid not being entirely honest (if that was what happened, I'm still not sure), but in this case the therapist decided to terminate the boy from the program.

Sure, we were having some problems with Parker. He'd lied to us and was clearly struggling with parts of the program, struggling with his own fucked-up desires that he didn't want but didn't know how to stop. But the level of these infractions didn't seem to rise to the level that other clients had been allowed to overcome. Parker's punishment felt to us like retaliation. His therapist felt deceived. Within a week, our foster son was kicked out of the program and placed in a lockdown facility.

It was, at least, another treatment program. Although it was located a day's drive from Portland, we visited Parker as often as we could. His mother didn't. For a while, he talked a lot about coming to live with us when he finally got out of the treatment facility. We didn't know what to say. We all knew that day was years away. But we already felt like his "forever family," and we wanted to know if having Parker live with us was a real possibility because we knew it was something we were open to if his mother would allow it.

We tried to raise this question with his parole officer, to just say that if he might be able to come live with us in five years we needed to know to plan for the possibility. If there wasn't a possibility of that, someone needed to tell Parker that wouldn't happen so he didn't spend the next few years counting on it.

This conversation sparked the beginning of the end of our contact with Parker. The parole officer responded very suspiciously. He wanted to know why we cared about the boy. He said, "No one likes this kid. No one's been able to bond with him. What's so special about you?" It was almost a challenge.

We couldn't tell him. We didn't know. We just had. We'd seen Parker as a boy rather than a monster. We'd seen a troubled boy, to be sure, but a boy nonetheless, a boy desperate for love. We'd been told that he'd offended female guards and correctional officers by leering at them. He'd never leered at Diane. He'd treated her like a mom from day one. She had an instant and enduring bond with him too. Some of her best times that year were sitting on the sofa watching *Penguins of Madagascar* with him, laughing their heads off. When his mother visited him, she kept him at arm's length, never quite bonding with him. Diane, on the other hand, dreamed of adopting him, and if you saw them on the street or at a ballgame, you would have no idea he wasn't her biological son.

I don't know why. I don't know what makes someone bond with one person and not another. We certainly hadn't bonded with every boy who came through our home. But even Ginger, our bitchy Chihuahua who doesn't like anyone, had bonded with this kid.

When the boys first moved into the house Ginger wouldn't have anything to do with them. She would sneer at them, show her teeth and growl if they came near. But eventually she warmed to a couple of the boys, and Parker was one of them. She adored him. She'd run to him when we went to visit him at the lockdown facility. She'd climb all over him and lick his face and let him pet her, and she'd roll over and show him her belly. When she shows me her belly and I try to pet her, she always nips at me. She never bit him.

I'm not trying to say Parker was a good person or that she sensed his soul was pure or anything. I don't believe dogs can just tell if someone is likely to do bad or do good. But I don't think Parker was evil. I believe he did some very bad things after some very bad things were done to him. I was able to know exactly what he'd done and what he was capable of doing and still see something in him to like.

If that makes me "special," then so be it. But it shouldn't mark me as suspect. Yet, that's exactly how the parole officer started treating us. He began to say things about Diane's work, about us as people that seemed to suggest that he now questioned our motives toward Parker. He insinuated that somehow working at a lesbian publication or being transgender meant we couldn't have real feelings for a kid.

Not long after this, Parker was moved again. He failed to follow the rules at his residential program and was sent back to general population at a detention facility—a prison, not a therapy program. No one would give us his address. His parole officer would no longer respond to our calls. His previous program said they weren't allowed to release any information to us.

He'll never know that we still think of him regularly. He'll never know that we still love him. He'll never know that we would've taken him into our home when he got out of jail.

Our experience with Parker was the last straw. It broke us. We left the program.

The timing corresponded with us moving out of the house we'd lived in, as it had been sold. But we could have moved into a multiple-bedroom apartment if we'd wanted to continue being proctor parents. But it had become too painful. This was our excuse to stop foster-parenting.

DIANE

Being a foster parent was probably one of the most fulfilling and most frustrating things I've ever done, and Jacob's not joking when he says it broke us. It broke my heart in the end. I can still tear up thinking about Parker, wondering where he is and who he has to believe in him. Every kid needs hope.

I grew to care for each child that came through our home, and sometimes I was happy to see them graduate from the program and go back to their biological parents. But more often I was just afraid for them, of what would happen as soon as they were in that environment again.

We couldn't change their home lives; we couldn't change that they were going back there. Almost all of the boys we had in our homes had been sexually abused before they had abused someone themselves, but if the person who had abused them wasn't adjudicated themselves or if the court system wasn't aware of who the abuser was, they weren't necessarily removed from the child's life. We had one kid, judging from the way he talked, who had been abused by a sibling but wouldn't admit it to anyone; when he was headed back home to his overbearing and overly intimate mother and (probably abusive) sibling, I could tell he was as worried as we were. But in the confines of the foster-care system, biological family reunification is almost always the number-one goal.

My mom was a foster kid in the 1960s. After she got pregnant at fourteen, her abusive mother kicked her out of the house so the foster system sent her to live with a nice middle-class couple, Alice and Norm, and their kids. She was only allowed to live with them until the baby was born (and given up for adoption), but she came to love them very much and stayed in touch with them well after I was born a few years later. They introduced her to a life outside poverty and abuse, a kind of life she hadn't experienced before, and I honestly believe the horrendous life my mom has led would have taken a different route had she been able to continue growing up under their roof. So I believe that foster parenting is a really important thing for us to do when we can.

Foster parenting was hard for me in some of the same ways as Jacob—especially with the program we were with—because we couldn't just tell the kids to go outside and play, because they had to be supervised at all times, even in our backyard. Jacob and I could never be alone unless we were sleeping. We had less time for sex and for ourselves as a couple. We could no longer share experiences like antiquing or going out to dinner because the kids had to be with us, and generally one kid walked with me and one with him. I could really see how couples with kids could easily lose the "us" in favor of the larger family goals. Not saying that's even wrong, but it is a difficult transition for a couple still madly, deeply in love.

But I had different frustrations as well. While Jacob was overwhelmed and frustrated on weekends that I was off in San Francisco and he was saddled with four teenage boys and couldn't let any one of them out of sight and sound, I was working insane hours trying to keep my staff happy and glued together and get out a magazine on a tight budget and at the same time feeling like I was missing out on everything at home. I would get envious of Jacob because he could devote his day to the kids, and he was envious of me because I got away from it all every few weeks.

I also was having trouble not being able to be myself in the program. The children's presence constantly reminded me that anyone is allowed to have biological children, and short of real, serious physical abuse, nobody is going to take that kid away. But as a foster (technically proctor) parent, I felt like we were always in danger of losing the kids—to their parents, to a different, "more suitable" foster family, back to the system. And part of that was because of who I was. The program was very accepting of same-sex couples, but I think it expected that those couples aren't going to be—for lack of a better phrase—super gay in their presentation, their homes, their lives. One by one, we were asked to tone things down, and, as usual, that request always started with me. First, no shirts with cleavage and no tank tops. Do you know how hard it is to find a blouse nowadays that shows absolutely no cleavage that will actually fit a woman with big boobs? But I tried. I adopted the cardigan in seven colors and transitioned into what I called my soccer-mom clothes. (The day after we left the program, all those clothes, save for the cardigans, went to the Goodwill.)

I still had a burlesque dance troupe (we didn't strip naked or anything, though we wore sexy, sometimes skimpy, outfits onstage), but I never changed clothes at home, let the boys see or hear about our performances, or let anyone ever see my costumes. We moved rehearsals out of my basement and into a private rental studio, we called my hour away every Sunday morning my "dance class," and we placed locks on our bedroom door so nobody could sneak in and look through any of my sexy stuff (or kill us while we slept, which was only ever a concern when one of the violent kids was with us for the weekend).

Once I had mastered the soccer-mom clothes, had learned to speak more softly, stop cursing, and adopt some of the language that the program liked us to use, then came concerns I hadn't expected.

One kid was placed with us because s/he was trans; the therapists had said they wanted to put him in our home because "he had gender issues" and they thought we'd know better how to deal with that. We were open to seeing what that meant, because very often something called "gender issues" just means a boy likes to play with girls toys, dress up in typically female clothing, or watch movies and TV shows aimed at teenage girls. Sometimes it means the kid is gay; very rarely, it means the child is transgender. Often in our culture it just means the kid is doing something his parents don't think is gender appropriate. So with this child, who I'll call Dani, it was clear that he felt female and identified female, but it took a while before s/he finally said to us, "I want to be a girl, I think I am a girl."

My main problem through all this was that they didn't want us to be out about Jacob himself being trans. I was shocked and concerned, and though we went along with it (and I think it backfired) it just felt wrong to pretend we were something we weren't. Because we had both been out since we were teenagers we felt awful trying to hide that part of our selves because, by not talking about him being trans, we couldn't talk about me ever being queer, and then essentially we were a heterosexual couple to the kids and the outside fostering world. When Parker came along, they were concerned about the number of books we had on LGBTQ issues or by gay, bi, trans authors, so they asked us to lock our book cabinets so Parker couldn't access the books. Since I think more kids should be reading this stuff, not less, if we want more understanding in tolerance in the world, I hated that subterfuge too.

In a way, though, it was the first time Jacob could be just a man—not a trans man, not a former lesbian, just a man—in the eyes of those around us. That, I think he enjoyed, and though it rendered me a bit invisible, I learned that my world didn't shatter when that happened. I did reassert myself, my identity, in other places during that time, so perhaps that helped me cope with the invisibility. Or maybe it was just that I had gone through a period of time when I would do anything to have a kid, and now that I was a parent, albeit a foster parent, I was willing to go to a lot of lengths to keep it going. Very occasionally during that time I still thought of trying to get pregnant, especially when I had to send the kids home to their "real" parents, but mostly raising the boys filled me up and fulfilled my need to parent.

And my time with Parker I wouldn't trade for the world. I feel like I got a condensed lifetime of parenting during the time he was with us. Also I got sheer, maddening heartbreak when he was sent away. I've considered fostering again since then, but each time I relive that loss, that powerlessness I felt, and I lean toward protecting myself.

We've talked since then about fost-adopt, a program where you adopt a kid or siblings through the foster system. Maybe it's something we'll do when we're older, but right now, I think I'm content to dote on my nieces and nephew.

It's been a very long, emotionally torturous ride since 2000, trying to get pregnant, adopt a child, raise other people's children, all the different ways we tried to fulfill my parental needs. I'm now at an okay spot where I can admit it: I don't have kids and I will never have kids. But I have something that might be even better, if I can just make sure to experience it in the moment. I do know for certain my frenzied attempts at childbearing are over, and that's a big relief.

My friend Athena is now in the midst of what I experienced more than a decade ago, the height of my quest and the period of time where I had a circle of lesbian friends who were all trying to get pregnant. Of that group, I'm the only one who doesn't have children now. One of my friends adopted, after pregnancy and surrogacy both failed, and the others all got pregnant through alternative insemination or in vitro fertilization. But I can recount not being a mother without sadness now. It just is what it is, and I'm finally okay with that.

Chapter Fifteen

What I Learned From Pink (And Fran Drescher)

DIANE

After I took a job at *The Advocate* magazine in Los Angeles, we moved to Southern California, and that was when it really hit me: I'd just left two of the cities I felt most at home in, along with friends who'd become a second family to me. I was really sad that after twenty years San Francisco (and, to a lesser extent, Portland) had become an indelible part of me, but it wasn't always that way.

The transition to L.A. was slow; the people are so very different, the culture greatly different from that of San Francisco. Often little things that I find shocking (that my building doesn't recycle, for example) will get me a dismissive hand wave from my colleagues, who roll their eyes and say, "That's San Francisco."

I've learned to shut up more often, to ask less of my surroundings, to enjoy the weather more, expect to be liked less.

Then I talked to two different women in one week who really made me think about the subject of kids again—Pink and Fran Drescher.

Pink, who we all know as an amazing artist in the music industry, is also a mother and has a great wild child. She's about ten years younger than I am.

She told me that everything changed for her when she had her daughter. That's something I've heard over the years from many different women, and I've always—well, for a long time I found it kind of terrifying. You know, the whole idea that you could have a baby and like, you know, lose your fucking mind and suddenly nothing else matters in the world except that baby.

But the older I get, the more I've started to wonder if maybe I'm missing something, missing the crucial point, like maybe having a kid doesn't turn parents into robotic moms or stepford wives. Maybe they authentically discover something the rest of us are missing, that raising a child is a higher purpose than the sort of the things I've dedicated my life to. That fear of that unknown has driven me a lot.

Fran Drescher was married for eighteen years, and then she got divorced when her husband came out as gay. She and her ex are still best friends and partners. Drescher now has a TV show, *Happily Divorced*, based on her real-life experience, but before that she had her own show, which she and her ex-husband Peter created when they were still married, called *The Nanny*. In *Happily Divorced* on TV Land, her character is a middle-aged woman starting over in the dating pool, a fifty-something woman who never had children. Fran hasn't had them in real life either.

When I interviewed her I said, "I really apologize because nobody should ask this, but do you ever fear that you're going to look back at some point and regret never having kids? I mean, do you have any regrets?"

I've been desperate to hear more childless or child-free women answer this question. Honestly, I have an in-law who has no kids and I always want to ask her, but if it brings up bad memories I would feel terrible. So I've never asked. But I asked Fran.

She replied, "Well, you know, there was a time in my forties actually when I was ready to have a child."

That was after she and Peter got divorced and she was in another relationship. But then she was diagnosed with cancer and it changed everything, of course, because she had to focus on fighting the cancer. I think it also changed her new relationship.

The point is, she was saying something like, "We make choices, and at some point you just have to say, 'This is the path

I've taken.' There's no point in looking back and thinking, 'What if,' because we all have different paths. And whatever your path is, that is your path. Those are the choices you've made, and you shouldn't feel bad about them."

Fran Drescher may be right that the path Jacob and I are on is our path, but I don't always feel like I'm on a path I chose.

Rather than feeling as if we've been at different crossroads and had to pick a direction, sometimes it has seemed more like we're navigating an enormous river in a tiny canoe. We paddle as hard as we can, but really, whether we go down one tributary or another has less to do with us and more to do with the current. We're just responding to the river and where it's taking us. We're just doing the best we can with the direction we've been pushed.

Fran also told me there will always be kids in this world that need mothering. Truthfully it reminds me that Jacob and I have raised children (foster kids), but whether we had kids of our own (either through adoption or birth) may just have never been in our hands. But we have seven nieces and one nephew all under the age of ten, and when we're with James, Ariana, Adrianna, Brianna, Lilyanna, Suttyn, Joanna, and Diana (yes, my namesake!), I couldn't be happier. However, I couldn't imagine having to take care of them all full-time either.

I took the job at Here Media for many reasons (being executive editor of the oldest LGBTQ publication in the country helped), but one of the biggest is so I could get closer to the kids. I find that very often my dreams of parenting, the moments I wish I could experience, aren't the day-to-day ones; they're the special days like Halloween or homecoming. As an aunt, I can be there for that. I can teach the kids to swim in the summer, spend a day feeding them candy and churros at Disneyland, videotape them re-creating Justin Bieber songs in the backyard. Then they can go home where their parents make and enforce all the rules.

When we bought a house earlier this year, I had very few criteria besides a pool and a bedroom for the kids. I'll decorate it and fill it with toys and game stations and put up their art in frames, and whenever the kids come over they'll have a place in our home that is theirs. I think that if I'm open to it, that arrangement may offer me the best of both worlds. Even better, my sister Wendy recently asked if Jacob and I would become godparents for her two girls. We were thrilled. So maybe being a godparent will be enough.

I don't know. We'll find out together.

JACOB (SUZY)

At some point in the past few years I was telling a therapist about our attempts to bring children into our lives.

She responded, "It sounds like you think that was some kind of personal failure."

"Yeah," I said, not understanding the confusion. "We failed. We failed to conceive, we failed to have the money for a private adoption, we failed to pass the fost-adopt program—we failed."

I think Fran Drescher and her husband Peter actually went through something similar to what we did, even though it was completely different as well. I'm not sure that I believe things work out the way they're supposed to or that we choose our paths or God only gives us as much as we can handle.

Am I at peace about not having kids?

Well, I still feel like forty-five is young enough that we can't truly rule anything out forever. Hell, I used to be a woman. Anything's possible.

But I do feel like spending more time with the nieces and nephews will be enough—at least for me. As we're finishing this book we've also taken another huge leap in our journey together: Diane and I just bought a house.

We chose a home located less than thirty minutes from all of our nieces and nephews. It has a spare bedroom—and a pool—for visiting kids. So I think we'll get plenty of time with the kids. I imagine we will, at times, be thrilled that they all have parents we can send them home to at the end of the day.

I've come to believe that one of the things that has kept us together is *not* having children. Becoming foster parents made me realize that being good parents means making the kid(s) the top priority. And when you do that, their need for attention can suck the life out of you. Really. They can drain all your energy until you're exhausted every night. They have a way of getting between the two of you, of becoming the center of attention, of turning you into asexual beings. It's not that kids aren't wonderful or that you won't both love them, or that you might stay together because of your shared commitment to your kids, but they will change your relationship with each other.

Overall, I'm delighted with how my life has turned out. I still wish I could conquer my pain problems and that we had more money and time to travel together and do other things we love (without the fear we'll be dumpster diving in retirement). But I wouldn't change the past—not even the difficult times—if it could alter the here and now.

I couldn't imagine sharing my life with anyone but Diane. She's my longtime companion, my co-conspirator, my copilot, my queerly beloved. I know the future will continue to hold unforeseen complications and distractions and scenic byways. But in our travels getting there has always been as important as being there. As long as we continue to enjoy the ride, I'm sure we'll be happy with our final destination.

EPILOGUE: WHAT KEEPS US TOGETHER

JACOB (SUZY)

I still remember the affair I had with a woman named Carol in Northampton before I met Diane. Carol told me she couldn't break up with her girlfriend because they owned a car together. I thought it was an excuse then. If she really loved me she'd find a way to split their shared possessions. Obviously they managed to do just that, because when I ran into Carol at the coffee shop around the corner from the *Girlfriends* office several years later, she and her girl were no longer a couple.

But that comment contained a truth, and that's why I recall it. Someone asked me recently what marriage meant to me, and I said that part of it is just a system of government subsidies that support a relationship and legally binding agreements that make it difficult to end said relationship. There's something to be said for making it inconvenient to break up. That's one reason I support marriage equality despite the institution's patriarchal origins that posited marriage as a business arrangement, one man passing ownership of his daughter to another man, who takes her as his wife, thus creating an environment for the protection of one's lineage.

Queer relationships have so much inherently stacked against them that they can use any help they can get. We all know that larger society—our churches, our birth families, our government—

doesn't support our relationships. They belittle them, dismiss them as inauthentic or immature in comparison with hetero couplings.

It's not that I really believe couples do or should stay together simply so they don't have to divide their assets. But every hurdle helps. You know, the easier it is to say good-bye, the more likely you'll march out the door in a fit of anger and never return. Sharing possessions, bank accounts, mortgage payments, one form of transportation, etc. makes separating difficult and hard to do overnight. The longer it takes to pull the two halves apart, the more likely they'll fuse back together before the connection has been broken. Not wanting to or even knowing how to separate your belongings, friends, and pets, all that helps keep you together, but other things you share also bind you together.

For all the times Diane and I've scoffed at romantic notions of "the one," (Diane always says imagine how sad the world would be if there was really only one) we've come to believe that we're uniquely paired. We're the only people who really understand each other, especially those parts of ourselves we don't share with the rest of the world. We can say things to each other, share our true feelings, even when they're perversely un-PC, and rather than being shocked or surprised or even just understanding, we often find that we actually share those secret leanings.

We really believe we were made for each other, that losing our relationship would be losing something central to ourselves.

What keeps us together? Sharing private jokes, quoting *The Simpsons*, saying one word or one sentence that references an entire experience. All our shared experiences build on each other, like geological layers in the Grand Canyon, until they add up to be more than what they are, greater than the sum of their parts. The things we both laugh at, the things we don't. The crazy stories we share, our tradition of no traditions. The pets we've raised, the grandparents we've lost.

Diane and I assume that we'll be here tomorrow, that neither of us is going away. We place our faith in another human being to hold our heart like a little mouse, tight enough that the other doesn't squeeze its flexible body out between fingers, but not too tight, not tight enough to smother or bruise or break. It's a huge trust to let someone else have that power over you.

All of us do it all the time, putting ourselves out there on dates and booty calls, looking for the right person for us. But it's so scary and you have to trust so much, and you have to fight off all of your own defense mechanisms, not pull up the drawbridge when you see the horde approaching, not shut the gate or defend the fortress but tear down your own walls, brick by brick removing the supports of your own tower on high. That step it takes to not back away from something frightful or revolting or disturbing but to look right at it and stand your ground is the key. That's what it feels like not to run, not to break up with each other, or, more accurately, not to push Diane to the point where she will break up with me.

Then we have that shared-brain thing, where we finish each other's sentences, where we're half as smart alone as we are together, where we seem to know what the other is thinking, where we can channel each other's voice in our writing.

She's always in my head, I'm always in hers. It's a good thing. After all, she is my queerly beloved.

THINGS YOU SHOULD KNOW ABOUT THIS BOOK

JACOB (SUZY)

1. Why we use the term "queer."

The title of this book, *Queerly Beloved*, was actually inspired by an episode of the animated Fox TV show, *The Simpsons*. When the town of Springfield is having financial problems, someone suggests they legalize same-sex marriages and capitalize on gay-wedding tourism. Not one to miss out on get-rich-quick schemes, Homer Simpson becomes an ordained minister and opens a chapel in his garage.

When officiating same-sex nuptials, Homer begins, "Queerly beloved, we are gathered here today…" It was done for laughs, but Diane and I latched on to it for different reasons.

Despite its widespread usage, the word "queer" is still controversial.

Some members of the lesbian, gay, bisexual, and transgender community object to the use of the term, which is—for them—forever tainted by negative connotations as a derogatory slur. Many straight people similarly have only heard it as a slur. Others, especially Gen-Xers like Diane and myself, have embraced the term, reclaiming it from the bigots and using it as an all-inclusive umbrella term for the diverse individuals who make up the LGBTQ community.

For us, the fact that Merriam-Webster defines "queer" as "differing in an odd way from what is usual or normal" and gives it the synonyms of "eccentric, unconventional, mildly insane, touched" is actually a positive thing.

We are proud of being different, weird, unconventional, unique. We both, even at forty-five years old, aspire to stick out rather than assimilate into an undifferentiated mass. (That's not to suggest we don't want the same rights as everyone else, because we do.)

The word "queer" has also been particularly useful in our relationship—which has survived two decades and my gender transition. In colloquial terms, I had a "sex change." That change occurred late in our relationship, after we'd been a lesbian couple for fifteen years.

Suddenly we weren't sure what to call our relationship, how to define ourselves, and whether we could still find a place in the community that had been not only our home but, as journalists who worked in the LGBTQ media, the basis of our professional lives as well.

We already saw ourselves as a queer couple. And instead of embracing a heterosexual or straight identity post-transition, we have continued to identify *as* queer. We will fight to the death for the right to do so, even as we understand others' desires to go stealth (and be seen as merely a heterosexual couple) or to eschew the word altogether (because, often, it was thrown at them as a youth, very often along with punches and psychological terror). We understand. Please understand us. (And yes, I too have been on the receiving end of one of those punches accompanied by name-calling.)

Queerly Beloved is the story of our relationship—and how it survived such a monumental change. But this book is about more than that. It is also about our other loves: the people, places, and periodicals that Diane and I have fallen in love with over the years and how those other queer loves have altered our journey as a couple.

This journey may reflect the experiences of other couples, but it is inherently a personal one. Our experiences are our own and should be in no way taken as representative of any other couple or person, be they transgender or cisgender or intersex, gay or straight or queer or bisexual, monogamous or polyamorous.

2. Who am I? Suzy or Jacob?

For many transgender people, talking about their past can be quite difficult, especially during or after their transition (which, despite what TV and film would have you believe, is rarely just one event but rather a long series of events and, for some, a lifetime of change and development). We wonder, how do you talk about the person you were beforehand? Do you use the name you were given at birth when you recall your childhood? Do you petition to have your childhood records and even your birth certificate itself retroactively amended to reflect your preferred sex and name?

I was born in 1967, in the state of Idaho, a state that does not allow transgender residents to amend their birth certificates. My birth certificate still lists me as female, still lists my given name, Susannah Christine Minshall. Idaho is one of the only states in the nation that will not let you amend your birth certificate after you've had surgery to become the correct sex.

Still, how we talk about ourselves in the past is, ultimately, a personal decision. I haven't thrown away my baby pictures. I haven't even thrown away the pictures that documented the two occasions in my life during which I wore a dress.

I recently told my mother she didn't have to get rid of the trappings of my youth. I'm not ashamed of my past. I was that child named Suzy.

Diane and I thought a lot about how to best address this question in terms of this book, *Queerly Beloved*. After much reflection, we decided not to use the name Jacob throughout because we think you, our readers, deserve to experience our story the way we experienced it. And before I came out as trans we experienced me as female. We experienced ourselves as a lesbian couple, and for the most part (when we were not being confused as sisters, say) the world experienced us as a lesbian couple.

This is not to say that I have always been comfortable with the female identity. Far from it. But after growing up as a tomboy and coming out as a butch lesbian feminist, I had begun to identify *as* female by the time Diane and I met and fell in love. In fact, for three-quarters of my life I have been known as a girl named Suzy. It is only in the last quarter that I have become known as a man named Jacob.

So, for the most part, we have used my coming out as the demarcation line to switch from referring to me as Suzy to calling me Jacob. This might have been a little confusing—I know the experience certainly was for us—but it seemed the truest way to tell our story.

To help you keep track of which of us is speaking, we headed our subsections by our names. Diane's pieces were under the heading DIANE, and mine were either under the heading JACOB (SUZY) or SUZY (JACOB). Whether an event occurred before or after my transition should have been apparent by which of my names was first and highlighted. The other name remained there in parentheses as a reminder that we are the same person. I am the same person.

A NOTE ABOUT TIME

JACOB (SUZY)

Diane and I perceive chronological time differently. This became clear almost immediately in our relationship, when we were first seeing each other but still lived in different cities.

When her weekend visits came to a close I would invariably complain about not seeing her for five days, and she would insist that it wasn't five days, but three.

She said I couldn't count Monday, because, even though it was insanely early when she left, she did see me on Monday. Diane said I also couldn't count Friday, because, even though it was often insanely late when she arrived, she did see me on Friday. So that left Tuesday, Wednesday, and Thursday. Three days.

From my accounting, Diane left before dawn Monday morning and didn't arrive until after dark Friday night, which meant five long days without her. We would be apart all day Monday, Tuesday, Wednesday, Thursday and Friday. Five days.

In counting our time apart, Diane always seemed to use this rounding-down system. But when she calculated our time together, she always seemed to round up.

At some point, within the first few years of our getting together, Diane began to say that we met in 1990, at Boise, Idaho's first Gay Pride. The day, the event, it was amazing, but was it 1990 or 1991? Was it the first or the second?

I disagreed, arguing that in the summer of 1990, I was still living in Northampton, Massachusetts and she was still living in New Orleans. But she insisted.

And at some point, within the first five years, I relented. Diane is often persuasive. It didn't seem to matter anymore whether it had been 1990 or 1991. So I started agreeing that, yes, we met in 1990. And we celebrated anniversaries based on the 1990 date. That made the year really easy to count from, being a nice round number and the beginning of a decade.

Years passed. Decades passed. We continued telling everyone our origination story, with our agreed-upon date of 1990.

That brings us to the present, the early months of 2014 as we are wrapping up, fact-checking, really, the finishing touches on this book. Suddenly the difference between 1990 and 1991 became apparent. We started our story in June of 1990 but soon ran into a problem.

When we began attaching dates to the other elements of our story, we began to see that they didn't seem to line up. We were missing a year.

If we insisted on keeping our anniversary date as we'd been calling it for over two decades, we would have to pad the story, stretch out the action and add twelve months.

Diane was very upset to discover I'd been misleading her all these years and causing her to inadvertently mislead the public in numerous articles, speeches, and essays. But, she complained, when it came to our story, keeping the date 1990 and adding a year would interrupt the flow of the narrative.

Plus, I said, it's not the truth.

Oh, right.

Which, I'm afraid, brings us to the "truth."

How did we decide what is true? How did we tell our true story?

We chose to use a style of writing called creative nonfiction. This allowed us the freedom to occasionally combine several events into one, to provide dialogue even when we didn't have transcripts to refer to, to add color and descriptions to scenes that may not be as vivid in our forty-something minds as they were when we experienced them as twenty-somethings.

However, creative fiction didn't allow us to lie. In other words, we could embellish our story, but it still had to be our story. We couldn't make things up or steal them from other people who have led more interesting lives. So, this is, to the best of our collective knowledge and memory, the truth.

But of course, like our experience of time, truth is somewhat subjective. I don't always remember things happening the way Diane does. Sometimes we out-and-out disagreed with each other about what happened when, what it meant, or how we reacted.

When those situations arose in writing this collaboration we used two methods to resolve disagreements. If the disagreement was slight, we compromised. We went with what seemed the more authentic and eloquent version of events. However, we thought sometimes our story was best told through each of our viewpoints. In those cases, we switched from one narrator to the other.

I told you my side of the story.

Then Diane told you what *really* happened.

About the Authors

Diane and Jacob Anderson-Minshall are co-conspirators in life and love. They co-author the Blind Eye mystery series (*Blind Curves*, *Blind Leap*, and the Lambda Literary Award finalist *Blind Faith*). *Queerly Beloved* is the true story of how the once lesbian couple survived a gender transition. Their 23-year-relationship has been the subject of numerous articles (including in *The New York Times*) and radio programs (like NPR's *Story Corp*).

Diane is editor at large of *The Advocate* magazine, editor in chief of *HIV Plus* magazine, and contributing editor to SheWired, OutTraveler, and Gay.net. She penned the erotic-thriller, *Punishment With Kisses*, and her writing has appeared in dozens of publications and anthologies. The couple co-founded *Girlfriends* magazine, and Diane also launched *Alice* magazine and previously served as the longtime editor in chief of *Curve* magazine. She has won numerous journalism awards, including a 2013 NLGJA award, and in 2014 will serve as a delegate to the United Nations Commission on the Status of Women. You can find her on Twitter @DeliciousDiane.

Jacob sits on the board of Lambda Literary Foundation. He has written for numerous LGBT and feminist publications and, for four years, he penned the nationally-syndicated weekly column, TransNation. He later produced and co-hosted the radio show, *Gender Blender*. His work is included in anthologies like *Men Speak Out: Views on Gender, Sex, and Power* (now in its 2nd edition) and the award-winning *Portland Queer*. In addition to his journalistic efforts, Jacob is also a mixed media artist and is at work on his first graphic novel. You can find him on Twitter @Jake2Point0.

You can find out more and contact them at www.Anderson -Minshall.com.

Books Available From Bold Strokes Books

Queerly Beloved: A Love Story Across Genders by Diane and Jacob Anderson-Minshall. How We Survived Four Weddings, One Gender Transition, and Twenty-Two Years of Marriage. (978-1-62639-062-1)

The Thief Taker by William Holden. Unreliable lovers, twisted family secrets, and too many dead bodies wait for Thomas Newton in London—where he soon enough discovers that all the plotting is aimed directly at him. (978-1-62639-054-6)

Waiting for the Violins by Justine Saracen. After surviving Dunkirk, a scarred and embittered British nurse returns to Nazi-occupied Brussels to join the Resistance, and finds that nothing is fair in love and war. (978-1-62639-046-1)

Turnbull House by Jess Faraday. London 1891: Reformed criminal Ira Adler has a new, respectable life—but will an old flame and the promise of riches tempt him back to London's dark side...and his own? (978-1-60282-987-9)

Stronger Than This by David-Matthew Barnes. A gay man and a lesbian form a beautiful friendship out of grief when their soul mates are tragically killed. (978-1-60282-988-6)

Death Came Calling by Donald Webb. When private investigator Katsuro Tanaka is hired to look into the death of a high profile lawyer, he becomes embroiled in a case of murder and mayhem. (978-1-60282-979-4)

Love in the Shadows by Dylan Madrid. While teaming up to bring a killer to justice, a lustful spark is ignited between an American man living in London and an Italian spy named Luca. (978-1-60282-981-7)

In Between by Jane Hoppen. At the age of fourteen, Sophie Schmidt discovers that she was born an intersexual baby and sets off on a journey to find her place in a world that denies her true existence. (978-1-60282-968-8)

The Odd Fellows by Guillermo Luna. Joaquin Moreno and Mark Crowden open a bed-and-breakfast in Mexico but soon must confront an evil force with only friendship, love, and truth as their weapons. (978-1-60282-969-5)

Cutie Pie Must Die by R.W. Clinger. Sexy detectives, a muscled quarterback, and the queerest murders...when murder is most cute. (978-1-60282-961-9)

Going Down for the Count by Cage Thunder. Desperately needing money, Gary Harper answers an ad that leads him into the underground world of gay professional wrestling—which leads him on a journey of self-discovery and romance. (978-1-60282-962-6)

Light by 'Nathan Burgoine. Openly gay (and secretly psychokinetic) Kieran Quinn is forced into action when self-styled prophet Wyatt Jackson arrives during Pride Week and things take a violent turn. (978-1-60282-953-4)

Baton Rouge Bingo by Greg Herren. The murder of an animal rights activist involves Scotty and the boys in a decades-old mystery revolving around Huey Long's murder and a missing fortune. (978-1-60282-954-1)

Anything for a Dollar, edited by Todd Gregory. Bodies for hire, bodies for sale—enter the steaming hot world of men who make a living from their bodies—whether they star in porn, model, strip, or hustle—or all of the above. (978-1-60282-955-8)

Mind Fields by Dylan Madrid. When college student Adam Parsh accepts a tutoring position, he finds himself the object of the dangerous desires of one of the most powerful men in the world—his married employer. (978-1-60282-945-9)

Greg Honey by Russ Gregory. Detective Greg Honey is steering his way through new love, business failure, and bruises when all his cases indicate trouble brewing for his wealthy family. (978-1-60282-946-6)